Joseph Pennell, Elizabeth Robins Pennell

An Italian pilgrimage

Joseph Pennell, Elizabeth Robins Pennell

An Italian pilgrimage

ISBN/EAN: 9783337291167

Printed in Europe, USA, Canada, Australia, Japan

Cover: Foto ©Lupo / pixelio.de

More available books at **www.hansebooks.com**

AN
ITALIAN PILGRIMAGE

BY

JOSEPH AND ELIZABETH ROBINS
PENNELL

Authors of "A Canterbury Pilgrimage"

LONDON
SEELEY & CO, 46, 47, & 48, ESSEX STREET, STRAND
(*Late of* 54, FLEET STREET)
1887

All Rights Reserved

To
Charles Godfrey Leland
*who is responsible
for our first Work
Together
&
who has been the Great Heart
of many a Pilgrimage
taken in his
Company
We
Dedicate this
Book.*

To

𝕿𝖍𝖊 𝕬𝖇𝖆𝖙𝖊 𝖉𝖎 𝕹𝖊𝖌𝖗𝖔

of

MONTE OLIVETO MAGGIORE
*We
would say a word of thanks
for
the Golden Days passed
in his House Beautiful
and for
the great kindnesses
shown us in our further
Journeying.*

PREFATORY NOTE.

THESE papers were originally published in the *Century*, the *Portfolio*, and *Outing*, the editors kindly allowing us to reprint and recast them. We hope readers who followed us from London to Canterbury may bear with us to the end of the Pilgrimage to Rome, of which our first journey was but the beginning. We warn them that the second stage, from Canterbury to Florence, has been ridden and written, but not yet wrought into a work.

JOSEPH PENNELL,
ELIZABETH ROBINS PENNELL.

3, *Castle Hill*,
   Lincoln.

STATIONS BY THE WAY.

	PAGE
THE START	1
IN THE VAL D'ARNO	5
AT EMPOLI	15
THE ROAD TO FAIR AND SOFT SIENA	18
AT POGGIBONSI	28
IN THE MOUNTAINS	31
FAIR AND SOFT SIENA	42
AN ITALIAN BY-ROAD	60
MONTE OLIVETO	83
THROUGH THE WILDERNESS TO A GARDEN	97
THE PILGRIMS ARE DETAINED IN MONTEPULCIANO	105
IN THE VAL DI CHIANA	113
LUCA SIGNORELLI'S TOWN	123
TO PERUGIA: BY TRAIN AND TRICYCLE	127

	PAGE
At Perugia	133
Across the Tiber to Assisi	140
At Assisi	145
Virgil's Country	150
Terni and its Falls	164
In the Land of Brigands	166
A Middling Inn	173
Across the Roman Campagna	175
The Finish	183
The Stones of Rome	187
Vetturino *versus* Tricycle	219

A Friend's *Apology*

For this Booke.

By Charles G. Leland.

Loe! what is this which *I'me to sett before ye?*
It is, I *ween, a very pleasant* Story,
How two young Pilgrimes *who the World would see,*
Did Wheele *themselves all over* Italy.
One *meant to write on't, whence it may be said*
That for the Nonce her's *was the Wheelwright's trade;*
Which is a clever Crafte, for yee *have heard*
What flits about as a familiar Word
Which in a Workshopp often meets the Eare,
" Bad Wheelwright maketh a good Carpentere.'
If of a bad one such a Saying's true,
Oh what, I *pray, may not a good one do?*

A Friend's Apology.

For by Experience I *do declare*
'*Tis easier to make Books than build a Chaire*,
Experto crede—I *have tried them Both*,
And sweare a Book is easier—on my *Oathe!*

He *who with* her *a* Pilgriming *did go*,—
That was her Husband. *As this Book doth show*,
Rare skill he *had when* he *would* Sketches *take*,
And from those Sketches prittie Pictures make.
She *with the* Pen *could well illuminate*,
He *with the* Pencil *Nature illustrate*.
Oh, is't not strange that what they *did so well*
In the Pen *way met in the Name* PEN-NELL ?
By which the Proverb doth approved appeare,
Nomen est Omen—*as is plaine and cleere.*
Which means to say that every Soule doth Bear
A name well suited to his charactere.

Now when this Couple *unto* Mee *did come,*
And askt me iff I'de *write a little Pome,*
That Tale and Picture as they *rouled along*
Might have some small Accomp'niment of Song,

A Friend's Apology.

I set my Pen to Paper with Delighte,
And quickly had my *Thoughts in Black and White,*
Even as JOHN BUNYAN *said he did of yore,*
So I, because I'd done the like before.
Since I was the first man of modern time,
Who on the Bicycle e'er wrote a Rime,
How I a Lady in a Vision saw
Upon a Wheel like that of Buddha's Law,
Which kept the Path and went exceeding fast ;
Loe ! now my Vision is fulfilled at last,
In this brave Writer who with ready Hand
Hath guided well the Wheel ore many a Land,
Showing the World by her *adventurous Course,*
How one may travel fast as any Horse
Without a Steed, and stop where'er ye will
And have for oats or stable nere a Bill.

As for the Rest—if you *but cast* your *Eye*
Upon the Pictures ere the Book ye *buy,*
And if of Art you *are a clever Judge,*
The Price for it you'll *surely not begrudge.*
Now, Reader, I *have praysed this Booke to* Thee,
I *trust that* Thou *wilt scan Itt carefullie ;*

A Friend's Apology.

'Twill set before Thee *Portraiture of Townes,*
Castles and Towres, antient Villes and Downs,
*How rowling Rivers to y*ᵉ *Ocean hast,*
Of Road side Inns and many a faire Palast,
Served up, I *ween, with so much gentle Mirthe,*
Thoulte *fairly own* thou'st *gott* thy *Money's Worth.*
If thou *art Cheated* Mine *shall bee the Sinn,—*
Turn o'er the Page, my Lady, *and Begin!*

Loe! Vanity Faire!—the Worlde is there,
   Hee and his Wife beside.
Ye may see it afoot, or from the Traine,
   Or if on a Wheel you ride.

AN ITALIAN PILGRIMAGE.

THE START.

"They are a couple of far countrymen, and after their mode are going on Pilgrimage."

WE stayed in Florence three days before we started on our pilgrimage to Rome. We needed a short rest. The railway journey straight through from London had been unusually tiresome because of our tricycle. From the first mention of our proposed pilgrimage, kind friends in England had warned us that on the way to Italy the machine would be a burden worse than the Old Man of the Sea. Porters, guards, and custom-house officials would look upon it as lawful prey, and we should pay more to get it to Italy than it had cost in the beginning. It is wonderful how clever one's friends are to discover the disagreeable, and then how eager to point it out!

Our first experience at the station at Holborn Viaduct seemed to confirm their warnings. We paid eight shillings to have the tricycle carried to Dover, porters amiably remarking that it would take a pile of money to get such a machine to Italy. Crossing the Channel, we paid five-and-sixpence more, and the sailors told us condolingly we should have an awful time of it in the custom-house at Calais. This, however, turned out a genuine seaman's yarn. The tricycle was examined carefully, but to be admired, not valued. "That's well made, that!" one guard declared with appreciation, and others playfully urged him to mount it. To make a long story short, our friends proved false prophets. From Calais to Florence we only paid nine francs freight and thirty-five francs duty at Chiasso.* But unfortunately we never knew what might be about to happen. We escaped in one place only to be sure the worst would befal us in the next. It was not until the cause of our anxiety was safe in Florence, that our mental burden was taken away.

But here were more friends who called our pilgrimage a desperate journey, and asked if we had considered what we might meet with in the way we were going. There was the cholera. But we represented that to get to Rome we should not go near the stricken provinces. Then they persisted that our road lay through valleys reeking with malaria until November at least. We should not reach these valleys before November, was our reply. Well then, did we know we must pass through lonely districts where escaped convicts roamed abroad; and in and out of villages where fleas

---

* This thirty-five francs duty *is said* to have since been abolished through the exertions of the National Cyclists' Union.

were like unto a plague of Egypt, and good food as scarce as in the wilderness? In a word, ours was a fool's errand. Perhaps it was because so little had come of the earlier prophecies that we gave slight heed to these. They certainly made no difference in our plans. On October 16th, the third morning after our arrival, we rode forth *sans* flea-powder or brandy, *sans* quinine or beef-extract, *sans* everything friends counselled us to take, and hence, according to them, right into the jaws of death.

IN THE VAL D'ARNO.

THE *padrone*, who helped to strap our portfolio and two bags to the luggage carrier, our coats to the handle bars and the knapsack to J——'s back, and Mr. Mead, the one friend who foretold pleasure, stood at the door of the Hotel Minerva to see us off. The sunlight streamed over the Piazza di Santa Maria Novella, and the beggars on the church-steps and the cabmen, who good-naturedly cried "No carriage for you!" as we wheeled slowly on over to the Via Tornabuoni; past Doni's; by Viessieux's; up the Lung' Arno to the crowded Ponte Vecchio, where for this once at least we were not attacked by the little shopmen; by the Via de' Bardi; then turning into the Borgo

San Jacopo; again along the Lung' Arno; and then around with the twisting street-car tracks, through the Porta San Frediano and out on the broad white road which leads to Pisa.*

But even before we left Florence we met with our first accident. The luggage carrier swung around from the middle to the side of the backbone. The one evil consequence, however, was a half-hour's delay. Beyond the gate we stopped at the first blacksmith's. Had either of us known the Italian word for wire, the delay might have been shorter. It was only by elaborate pantomime we could make our meaning clear. Then the blacksmith took the matter in his own hands, unstrapped the bags, and went to work with screw-driver and wire, while the entire neighbourhood, backed by passing pedlars and street-car drivers and citizens, pronounced the tricycle "beautiful!" "a new horse!" "a tramway!"

* The direct road to Rome starts from the Porta Romana.

When the luggage-carrier was fastened securely, and loaded again, the blacksmith was so proud of his success that he declared "nothing" was his charge. But he was easily persuaded to take something to drink the *Signore's* health. After this there were no further stops.

Our road for some distance went over streets laid with the great stones of the old Tuscan pavement,*—and for tricyclers these streets are not very bad going—between tall grey houses, with shrines built in them, and those high walls which radiate from Florence in every direction, and keep one from seeing the gardens and green places within. Women, plaiting straw, great yellow bunches of which hung at their waists, and children greeted us with shouts. Shirtless bakers their hands white with flour, and barbers holding their razors, men with faces half shaved and still

---

* Cycling, except under certain restrictions, is now forbidden in Florence. There is a cycling club in the Cascine.

lathered, and others with wine-glasses to their lips, rushed to look at this new folly of the foreigner, for ours was the first tandem tricycle ever seen in Italy. At Signa, on the steep up-grade just outside the town, we had a lively spurt with a dummy engine, the engineer apparently trying to run us down as we were about to cross the track. After this we rode between olives and vineyards where there were fewer people. There was not a cloud in the sky, so blue overhead and so white above the far hill-tops on the horizon. The wind in the trees rustled gently in friendliness. Solemn, white-faced, broad-horned oxen stared at us sympathetically over the hedges. One young peasant even stopped his cart to say how beautiful he thought it must be to travel in Italy after our fashion. All day we passed grey olive-gardens and green terraced hill-sides, narrow Tuscan-walled streams, dry at this season and long rows of slim, straight poplars,—white trees, a woman told us was

In the Sunlight.

their name. Every here and there was a shrine with lamp burning before the Madonna, or a wayside cross bearing spear and scourge and crown of thorns. Now we rode by the fair river of Arno, where reeds grew tall and close by the water's edge, and where the grey-green mountains rising almost from its banks were barren of all trees save dark stone-pines and towering cypresses, like so many mountains in Raphael's or Perugino's pictures. Now we came to where the plain broadened and the mountains were blue and distant. Mulberries, the peasants had stripped of their leaves before their time, but not bare because of the vines festooned about them, broke with their even ranks the monotony of grey and brown ploughed fields. Here on a hill was a white villa or monastery, with long lofty avenue of cypresses; there, the stanch unshaken walls and gates of castle or fortress, which, however, had long since disappeared. It is true all these things are to be seen hastily from the windows of the railroad train. But it is only by following the windings and long straight stretches of the road as we did, stopping now and then or riding slowly, th its great loveliness can be felt and known, as it must have been by the men of old, who understood so well how to make beautiful their longest journeys. Later in the afternoon, with a turn of the road, we came suddenly in view of Capraia, high up above, and far to the other side of the river; so far, indeed, that all detail was lost, and we could only see the mass of its houses and towers and *campanile*, washed into the whitish-blue sky. And all the time we were working just hard enough to feel that joy of mere living which comes with healthy out-of-door exercise, and, I think, with nothing else.

Sometimes we rode, seeing no one and hearing no other sound than the low cries of a cricket in the hedge or the loud calls of an unseen ploughman in a neighbouring field.

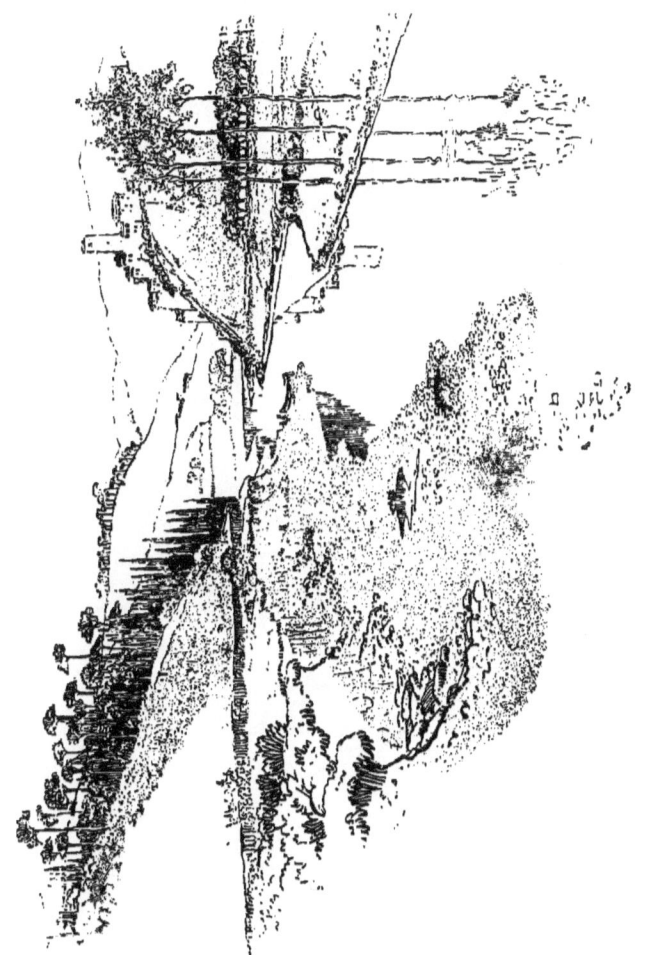

A Perugino Landscape.

Then an old woman went by, complimenting us on going so fast without a horse; and then a baker's boy in white shirt and bare legs, carrying a lamb on his shoulders. But then, again, we met wagon after wagon, piled with boxes and baskets, poultry and vegetables, and sleeping men and women, and with lanterns swinging between the wheels;—for the next day would be Friday and market-day, and peasants were already on their way to Florence. There were pedlars, too, walking from village to village, selling straw fans and gorgeous handkerchiefs. Would not the *Signora* have a handkerchief? one asked, showing me the gayest of his stock. For answer I pointed to the bags on the luggage-carrier and the knapsack on J——'s back. Of course, he said. We already had enough to carry. Would the *Signora* forgive him for troubling her? And with a polite bow he went on his way.

We came to several villages and towns,—

some small, where pots and bowls, fresh from the potter's wheel, were set out to dry ; others large, like Lastra, with heavy walls and gates, and old archways, and steps leading up to crooked, steep streets, so narrow that the sun never shines into them ; or like Montelupo, where for a while we sat on the bridge without the farther gate, looking at the houses which climb up the hill-side to the cypress-encircled monastery at the top. Women were washing in the stream below, and under the poplars on the bank a priest in black robes and broad-brimmed hat walked with a young lady. But whenever we stopped, children from far and near collected around us. There were little old-fashioned girls, with handkerchiefs tied over their heads in womanly fashion, who kept on plaiting straw, and small boys nursing big babies, their hands and mouths full of bread and grapes. If, however, in their youthful curiosity they pressed upon us too closely, polite men and women, who had also come

Street in Lastra.

to look, drove them back with terrible cries of *Via, ragazzi!* (go away, children!), before which they retreated with the same speed with which they had advanced.

Just beyond Montelupo, when a tedious up-grade brought us to a broad plateau, a cart suddenly came out a little way in front of us from a side road. A man was driving, and on the seat behind, and facing us, were two nuns who wore wide straw hats, which flapped slowly up and down with the motion of the cart. When they saw us, the younger of the two covered her face with her hands as if she thought us a device of the devil. But the other, who looked the Lady Abbess, met the danger bravely and sternly examined us. This close scrutiny reassured her. When we drew nearer she wished us good evening, and then her companion turned and looked. We told them we were pilgrims bound for Rome. At this they took courage, and the spokeswoman begged for the babies they cared for in Florence. We gave her a few sous. She counted them quite greedily, and then—but not till then—benevolently blessed us. They were going at jog-trot pace, so that we soon left them behind. "*Buono viaggio*," the Abbess cried, and the silent sister smiled, showing all her pretty white teeth, for we now represented a temptation overcome.*

* Road from Florence to Empoli, good.

AT EMPOLI.

WE put up that night at Empoli. The Albergo Maggiore was fair enough, and, like all large Italian inns had a clean, spacious stable in which to shelter the tricycle. The only drawback to our comfort was the misery at dinner of the black-eyed, blue-shirted waiter at our refusal to eat a dish of birds we had not ordered. He was very eager to dispose of them. He served them with every course, setting them on the table with a triumphant cry of *Ecco!* as if he had prepared a delicious surprise. It was not until he brought our coffee that he despaired. Then he retired mournfully to the kitchen, where his loud talk with the *padrona* made us fear their wrath would fall upon us or the tricycle. But later they gave us candles, and said good-night with such gracious smiles that we slept the sleep which knows neither care nor fear.

The next morning their temper was as unclouded as the sky. They both watched the loading of the tricycle with smiling interest. He had seen many a *velocipede* with two wheels, the waiter said, but never one with three. And that a *Signora* should ride, the *padrona* added, ah! that indeed was strange! Then she grew confidential. Only occasionally I caught her meaning, for my knowledge of Italian was small. She had had seven children, she said, and all were dead but one. And I, had I any? And where had I bought my dress? She liked it so much, and she took it in her hand and felt it. Should we stay long in Italy? and some time we would come back to Empoli? Her son, a little fellow, was there too. He had been hanging

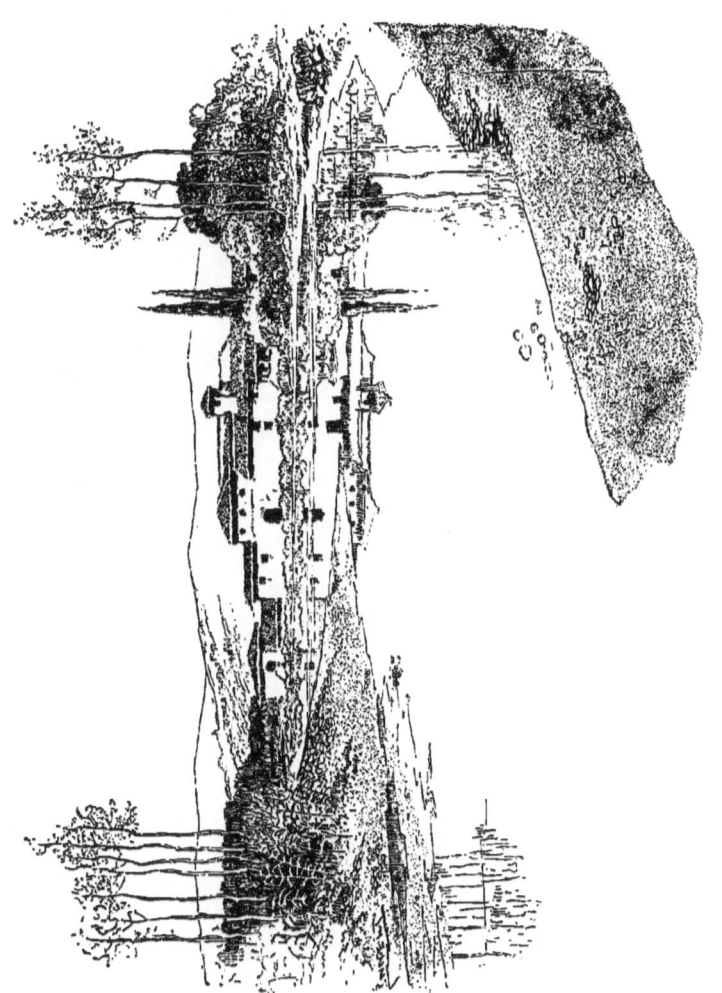

On the Arno, near Empoli.

about the machine when we came down to breakfast and ever since. He stood speechless while J—— was by, but when the latter went away for a few minutes—less shy with me I suppose because he knew I could not understand him as well—he asked, what might such a *velocipede* cost? as much perhaps as a hundred francs? But J—— coming back he was silent as before. They all followed us out to the street, the *padrona* shaking hands with us both, and the boy standing by the tricycle to the very last.

THE ROAD TO
FAIR AND SOFT SIENA.

It was good to be in the open country again, warming ourselves in the hot sunshine. The second morning of our ride was better than the first. We knew beforehand how beautiful the day would be, and how white and smooth was the road that lay before us. The white oxen behind the ploughs, and the mules in their gay trappings and shining harness, seemed like old acquaintances. The pleasant good morning given us by every peasant we met made us forget we were strangers in the land. A little way from Empoli we crossed the Ponte d'Elsa, and then, after a sharp turn to the right, we were on

At the Foot of the Cross.

the road to "fair and soft Siena." It led on through vineyards and wide fields lying open to the sun, by sloping hill-sides and narrow, winding rivers, by villas and gardens where roses were blooming. In places they hung over the wall into the road. We asked a little boy to give us one. For the *Signora*, J—— added. But the child shook his head. How could he? The roses were not his, he said. Once we passed a wayside cross on which loving hands had laid a bunch of the fresh blossoms. Sometimes we heard from the far-away mountains the loud blasting of rocks and then the soft bells of a monastery; sometimes the cracking of the whip of a peasant behind us, driving an unwilling donkey. Then we would pass from the stillness of the country into the noise and clamour of small villages, to hear the wondering cries of the women to which we were already growing accustomed, the piercing yells of babies, who, well secured in basket go-carts, could not get to us quickly enough, and the sing-song repetition of older children saying their lessons in school, and whom we could see at their work through the low windows.

About noon we rode into Certaldo, Boccaccio's town. I know nothing that interferes so seriously with hero-worship as hunger. I confess that if some one had said, "You can go either to see Boccaccio's house, or to lunch at a *trattoria*, but both these things you cannot do," our answer would have been an immediate order for lunch. We went at once to a *trattoria* on the piazza where Boccaccio's statue stands. I doubt if that great man himself ever gathered such numbers about him as we did. Excited citizens, when the tricycle was put away, stood on the threshold and stared at us until the door was shut upon them. Then they pressed their faces against the windows and peered over piles of red and yellow pears, and every now and then one, bolder than the rest, stealthily thrust his head in and then scampered off before he could be captured. This gave a spice of novelty and excitement to our midday meal.

We ordered a very simple lunch; soup, bread and cheese, coffee and vermouth. But the *padrona* had to send out for everything. Her sister, a young girl as fair as an Englishwoman, was her messenger. We were scarcely seated before she came back with coffee and a large bottle which she set before us. This of course was the vermouth, and we half filled our glasses and at once drank a little. The two women stared with a surprise we could not understand. The fair girl now disappeared on a second foraging expedition and stayed away until we had finished our soup. "*Ecco, vermouth!*" she said on her return putting another bottle in front of us. Then we knew the reason of their wonder. We had swallowed, like so much water, the not over strong cognac intended only to flavour our coffee. Presently the *padrona* entered into conversation with us. We were English, she supposed. No, Americans, we told her. At this there was great rejoicing. They had a brother in America. He lived in a large town called Buenos Ayres, where he kept a *trattoria*. Like theirs it was the *Trattoria Boccaccio*. They were glad to see any one from the same country, whether from North or South. Was it not all America? The *padrona* went up stairs to bring down his picture that we might see it. Her sister pointed to the purple woollen jersey she wore and said with pride her brother had sent it to her. It too was American. They even called in their old mother that she might see her son's fellow-countrymen.

We spent an hour wandering through the old town on top of the hill in which Boccaccio really lived. The sun was shining right down into the streets in which the gay kerchiefs of the women, the bunches of straw at their waists, and their cornstalk distaffs made bright bit of colour. Though we left the tricycle at the *trattoria*, our coming made a stir in the upper town. Our clothes were not like unto those of the natives, and J——'s knee-breeches and long black stockings made them wonder what manner of priest he might be. As we stood looking at the *loggia* and tower and arched doorway of Boccaccio's house, the custodian with a heavy bunch of keys came to take us through it. But we declined his services. We cared more for the old streets and walls and palaces, which, though their greatness has gone, have not been changed since mediæval times, than for an interior, however fine, whose mediævalism dates from to-day. The old man turned away rather sulkily. J—— seeing there had been some mistake, explained that we had not sent for him. Then his face cleared. The women had said we wanted him, else he would never have disturbed us, and he took off his hat and this time went away with a friendly *a rivederle*.

The Palazzo Communale, at the highest point of the town, is still covered with the arms and insignia of other years, of the Medici and Piccolomini, of the Orsini and Baglioni. Its vaulted doorway is still decorated with frescoes of the Madonna, and saints and angels. But everywhere the plaster is falling away, and in the courtyard grass grows between the bricks of the pavement, and instead of pages and men-at-arms we there saw only a little brown-faced ragged child climbing cat-like over the roofs, and a woman scolding him from below. We left the town by the city gate, through which we saw the near hills grey, bare, and furrowed, the long lines of cypresses, the stretches of grey olives, the valley below with its vineyards, and the far mountains, purple and shadowy, the highest topped with many-towered San Gimignano.

It is better not to be jocund with the fruitful grape in the middle of the day when one is tricycling. The cognac we had taken at lunch,

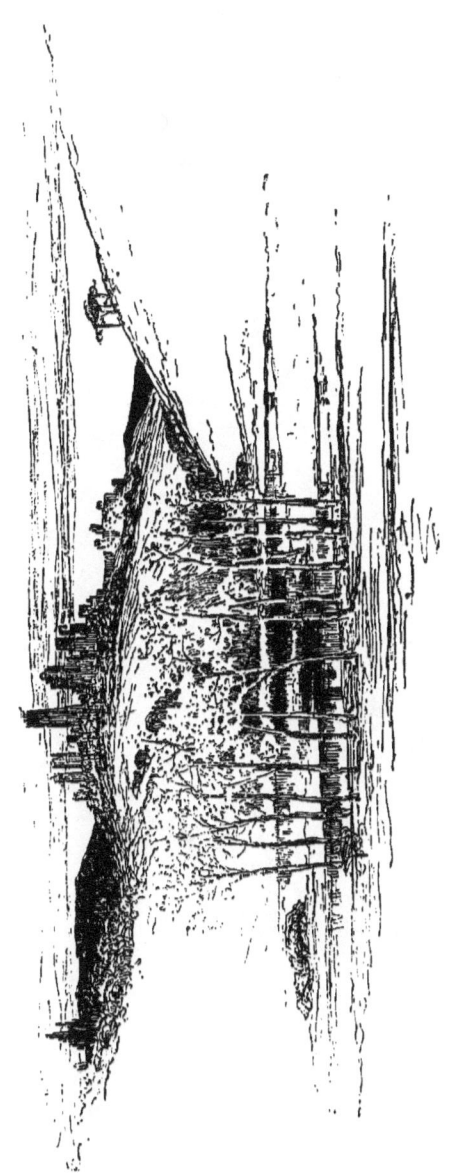

San Gimignano delle belle Torre.

weak as it was, and the vermouth made us sleepy and our feet heavy. I sympathised with the men who lay in sound slumbers in every cart we met. But their drowsiness forced us into wakefulness. Of the ride from Certaldo to Poggibonsi, I remember best the loud inarticulate cries of J—— and his calls of "*Eccomi!* as if he were lord of the land, to sleeping drivers. The Italian cry of the roads, rising to a high note and then suddenly falling and ending in a low prolonged one, which is indispensable to travellers, is not easy to learn. J——'s proficiency in it, however, when he limited himself to howling, made him pass for a native. But often donkeys darted into ditches and oxen plunged across the road before the peasants behind them awoke. Like Sancho Panza they had a talent for sleeping.

Once, after we had climbed a short but steep hill and had passed by several wagons in rapid succession, we stopped in the shade to take rest. It was a pleasant place. We looked over the broad valley, where the vines were festooned, not as Virgil saw them, from elm to elm, but from mulberry to mulberry, and up to San Gimignano, beginning to take more definite shape on its mountain-top. A peasant in peaked hat and blue shirt, with trousers rolled up high above his bare knees, crossed the road and silently examined the tricycle. "You have a good horse," he then said; "it eats nothing." We asked him if they were at work in his vineyard. No, he answered; but would we like to look in the wine-press opposite? And then he took us through the dark windowless building, where on one side the grape-juice was fermenting in large butts, and on the other fresh grapes had been laid on sets of shelves to dry. He picked out two of the finest bunches and gave them to me. When I offered to pay him he refused. The *Signora* must accept them, he said.

As the road was now a dead level and lumpy into the bargain we were glad when

San Gimignano.

Poggibonsi was in sight. We drew up on a bridge, where a man was standing, to ask him if he knew of a good inn. He recommended the Albergo dell' Aquila. "It is good," he went on, "and not too dear. This is not a town where they take one by the neck," and he clutched his own throat. So to the Albergo dell' Aquila we went. We had only to ride through the wide avenue of shady trees, past a row of houses, out of one of which a brown-robed monk came, to rush back at sight of us, past a washing-place surrounded by busy chattering women, and we were at the door of the inn.

AT POGGIBONSI.

THE inn was even more comfortable than the Albergo Maggiore in Empoli. We dined in a room from whose walls King Humbert and his queen smiled upon us, while opposite were two sensational and suggestive brigands in lonely mountain passes.

The *padrona* came up with the salad, and she and the waiter in a cheerful duet catechised us after the friendly Italian fashion, and then told us about the visit to their house of the American consul from Florence, of the hard times the cholera had brought with it for all Italy, of the bad roads to San Gimignano and the steep ones to Siena, along which peasants never travelled without bearing in mind the old saying: "*All' ingiù tutti i santi ajutano; ma all' insù ci vuol Gesù.*" ("Going down hill, call upon the saints; but going up one needs Jesus.") Before long J—— joined in the talk, and the duet became a trio. Never had I been so impressed with his fluent Italian. Even the *padrona* was not readier with her words than he with his. When I spoke to him about it afterwards, he said he supposed it was wonderful; he had not understood half of it himself.

After dinner and in the twilight we walked through the lively crowded streets and into the church, where service was just over. A priest in white surplice left the altar, and another began to put the lights out when we entered. But in the unlit nave many of the faithful still knelt in prayer. The town grew quieter as night came on, but just as we were going to sleep some men went along the street below our window singing. One in a loud clear tenor sang the tune; the others the accompaniment like a part song, and the effect was that of a great guitar. Their song was a fitting good-night to a day to whose beauty there had been not a cloud.

IN THE MOUNTAINS.

Though we left Poggibonsi in the beginning of the morning, a large crowd waited for us at the door of the inn. The *padrona* said farewell with many good wishes; men and women we had never seen before called out pleasantly *a rivederle*, two *carabinieri* watched us from the other side of the piazza, the railroad officials at the station cried, *Partenza! Partenza!* and then we were off and out of the town.

It would be *su, su, su* all the way, they told us at the inn, but for several miles we went fast enough, so that I felt sure the peasants we passed were still only calling on the saints. The ascent at first was very gradual, while the road was excellent. There were down as well as up grades, and for every steep climb we had a short coast. Now we came out on villas which but a little before had been above us, and now we reached the very summit of hills from which we looked forth upon mountain rising beyond mountain —some treeless and ashen grey, others thickly wooded and glowing with golden greens and russets, and still others white and mist-like, and seeming to melt into the soft white clouds resting on their highest peaks. All along, the hedges were covered with clusters of red rose-berries and the orange berries of the pyracanthus. The grass by the roadside was gay with brilliant crimson pinks, yellow snapdragons, and dandelions, and violet daisies. Once we came to a vineyard where the ripe fruit still hung in purple clusters from the vines, and where men and women, some on foot and others on ladders, were gathering and filling with them large buckets and baskets.

At the far end of the field white oxen, their great heads decorated with red ribbons, stood in waiting. Boys with buckets slung on long poles were coming and going between the vines. In all the other vineyards we had passed the vintage had been over, so we waited to watch the peasants, as, laughing and singing, they worked away. But when they saw us, they too stopped and looked, and one man came down from his ladder and to the hedge to offer us a bunch of grapes.

The only town through which we rode was Staggia, where workmen were busy restoring the old tower and making it a greater ruin than it had ever been before. One town gate has gone, but from the battlements of the other grass and weeds still wave with the wind, while houses have been built into the broken walls. It is a degenerate little town, and its degeneracy, paradoxical as it may sound, is the result of its activity. For its inhabitants have not rested content like those of Lastra with the mediævalism that surrounds them. They have striven to make what is old new by painting their church and many of their houses in that scene-painting style which to-day seems to represent the art of the people in Italy. Often during our journey we saw specimens of this vile fashion—houses with sham windows and shutters, churches with make-believe curtains and cords—but nowhere was it so prominent as in Staggia.

Beyond Monteriggione, whose towers alone showed above its high walls, the road began to wind upward on the mountain-side. It was such a long, steady pull that although the surface was perfect we gave up riding and walked. Our machine was heavily loaded and not too easy to work over prolonged up-grades. Besides, we were not time nor record makers nor perambulating advertisements, and we had the day before us. We were now closed in with woods; on either side were chestnuts and dwarf oaks and bushes, their leaves all "yellow and black and pale and hectic red." And occasional openings showed near mountain-tops covered with downy grey grass and a low growth like heather, and here and there were groups of dark pines. For an hour at least we were alone with the sounds and silence of the mountains. The wandering wind whispered in the wood, and black swine rooted in the fallen leaves, but of human life there was no sign. Then there came from afar a regular tap-tap, low at first, but growing louder and louder, until, as we drew closer to it, we knew it to be the steady hammering of stone-breakers. There were two men at work in this lonely pass, and as we stood talking to them two more came from under the chestnuts. These had guns on their shoulders, and wore high boots and the high-crowned conventional brigand hat. Ever since we left Florence we had seen at intervals in the fields and woods a notice with the words, "*È vietata la bandita,*" which we had interpreted as a warning against the bandits or convicts for whom our Florentine friends had prepared us. And now we seemed to have come face to face with two of these brigands. But it turned out there was little of the bandit about them save their appearance. Their guns were for birds, and later on we learned that the alarming signs were merely to forbid the trespassing of these very gentlemen.

A mile or two further on the road began to go down again. We were both glad to be on the machine after our walk. We could see to the bottom of the hill, and there was no one in sight. J—— let go the brake. None but cyclers know the delight of a five minutes' coast after hours of up-hill toiling. They, however, will sympathise with our pleasure in the mountains near Siena. But when it was at its fullest, and the machine was going at the rate of about twenty miles an hour, and neither brake nor back-pedalling could bring it to a sudden halt, a man, or the foul fiend him-

A slight obstruction.

self, drove a flock of sheep out from the woods a few feet in front of us. When we reached them only the first had crossed the road. Of course, all the rest had to follow. They tried to go on right through the wheels, but only succeeded in getting under them, setting the machine pitching like a ship in a heavy sea. But I held on fast, J—— stood on the pedals and screwed the brake down, the little wheel scattered the sheep like the cow-catcher of an engine, and we brought up in the gutter. Before we stopped J—— began a moral lecture to the shepherd, and was showing him how if the machine had gone over, the consequences would have been worse for us than for his flock. The lecture ended rather *un*morally with *Accidente voi*, and *Imbecile*, the deadliest of all Italian maledictions, punishable in places by imprisonment. The shepherd looked as if he was ready to curse us in return, but before he had time to form an expression suitable to the occasion, we were out of hearing, though we first made sure that no sheep were hurt. We were none the worse for the accident, and the tricycle was uninjured, save for a deep dent in the dress guard.

The rest of our way was divided between walking and riding. The woods with their solitude and wildness—but not the good road—came to an end. Once beyond them we wheeled out by fields where men and women were at work, their oxen whiter than any we had yet seen by contrast with the rich red of the upturned earth. In olive-gardens peasants were eating their mid-day meal; men with white aprons, women with enormous Sienese hats, and dogs and oxen were all resting sociably together. By the roadside others were making rope, the men twisting and for ever walking backwards, a small boy always turning at the wheel. Scattered on the hill-tops and by the road were large red-brick farm-houses, instead of the white ones we had seen near Florence.

Noontide.

At one where there was a well on the other side of the wall, we asked for a glass of water. A man brought it to the gate, where he was joined by three or four others. They stared inquiringly at the tricycle, at the bags and at us while J—— squeezed lemon juice into the water. Then one opened his mouth very wide and pointed to his teeth: "The little sir," he asked, "is he a dentist?" And so we were taken for an advertisement after all. Only the evening before we had seen at Poggibonsi by many posters that a travelling dentist was to pass that way.

It was noon when we first saw Siena, and we were then at the very walls. In the old days it was always said, "More than her gates, Siena opens her heart to you!" But the heart of him who sat in office by the city gate was shut against us. When we rode past him he bade us descend. To our "*Perchè?*" he said it was the law. Oh the vanity of these Sienese! Through the streets of Florence and over the crowded Ponte Vecchio we had ridden undisturbed, but in this mountain town, which boasts of but two hacks, and where donkeys and oxen are the only beasts to be frightened, we were forced to get down. The dignity of the law-makers of the city must be respected! So we two weary pilgrims had to walk along the narrow streets, between the tall palaces, while tanners in red caps, and women in flowered, white-ribboned hats, and priests and soldiers stared, and one man, with a long push-cart, kept close to us like an evil genius in a dream. He was now on one side and now on the other, examining the wheels, asking endless questions, and always getting in the way. At all the street corners he hurried on before, and with loud shouts called the people to come and see. Then he was at our heels again, shrieking his loud, shrill trade cry into our very ears. J—— as a rule is not ill-tempered; but there is a limit to all things. The stupid sheep, the watchful guard, and now this plague of a flower-pedlar brought his patience to an end, and on our way through the town he said much in good plain English which it was well the citizens could not understand.

FAIR AND SOFT SIENA.

EVEN pilgrims of old, on their way to Rome, sometimes tarried in castle or village. We could not pass through Siena, discourteous though her first welcome had been, as we had through smaller and less fair towns. So for a day or two we put away our tricycle, and the "cockle-shells and sandal shoon" of our pilgrimage. We went to a *pension*, one at which J—— had stayed before, and which he liked. I admit it was better in many ways than the inns in which we had hitherto slept and eaten. There was carpet on the floor of our room, and in it easy-chairs and a lounge. There were elaborate breakfasts at one and still more elaborate dinners at six, and there was always a great plenty, as the Englishwoman who sat next to me, and who, I fear, had not always fared so well, said, when she urged me to eat and drink more of the fruit and wine set before me. "You can have all you want in this house," she finished with a sigh, as if her crown of sorrow was in remembering *unhappier* things. But we both thought regretfully of the dining-rooms with the bad prints on the walls, and the more modest dinners of our own ordering. I think, too, we had found more pleasure in the half-understood talk of *padroni* and waiters than we did now in the elegant and learned conversation of our fellow-boarders, for they were all, it seemed, persons of learning and refinement. There was the retired English major-general who sat opposite, and who had written a book, as he very soon let us know. He recognised us as Americans before we opened our mouths to speak, which fact he also let us know by his reminiscences addressed not to us, but to our neighbours. He had travelled in Spain with

Mr. Fillmore, the ex-President, "the most courteous of gentlemen." He said he well knew Mr. Marion Crawford, the talented novelist, and his uncle, "dear old Sam Ward." He had counted among his best friends Ba-yard Taylor, "as you remember I have said in my book." This same book which made the major so communicative appeared to have crushed the spirit out of his wife, who sat silent during dinner. Then there was the elderly English lady travelling abroad with her daughter, who "has just taken up architecture," she informed us; "she has always painted heads till now, but she is *so* fascinated by her architectural work. Then I, you know, am *so* fond of water colours." And there was the Swedish lady, who could talk all languages, speaking to us in something supposed to be English, and who was as eager in her pursuit of food for her body as for her mind. I count the way in which she greedily swallowed the *vino santo* in her glass, when our host passed around the table the second time with his precious bottle, one of the wonders of our visit to Siena. It was pathetic too to see her disappointment when he turned away, just before he reached her, his bottle empty. And there were still others who knew much about pictures and palaces, statues and studios, and no doubt we might greatly have profited thereby; but we liked it better up stairs, where we were alone and there was less culture. Our window overlooked a high terrace in which marigolds and many-coloured chrysanthemums were blooming, the gardens of the Piccolomini Palace full of broad-leaved fig-trees and pale olives, and the wide waste of mountain and moorland stretching from the red city walls to the high, snow-capped Apennines on the horizon. All the morning the sun shone in our windows, and every hour and even oftener we heard the church bells, and the loud, clear bugle-calls from the barracks, once a monastery, whose mass of red and grey walls rose from the near olives. They say it snows in Siena in the winter-time, and that it is cold and bleak and dreary, but I shall always think of it as a place of flowers and sunshine and sweet sounds.

But best of all were the hours when we wandered through the town, up and down dark alley-ways and flights of steps, under brick arches, along precipitate, narrow streets, where we had to press close to the houses, or retreat into an open door, to let the wide-horned oxen pass by with their load; now coming out at the very foot of La Mangia, on the broad, sunny *piazza;* now by the tanneries, where little streams of brown water trickled down towards the washing-place at the foot of the hill, and where the walls were hung with dripping brown skins, probably just as they were when the little Catherine, her visions already beginning, and Stefano walked by them and towards home in the fading evening light, from a visit to the older and married sister Bonaventura.

One hour we were with the past in the shadowy aisles of the *Duomo*, where Moses and Hermes Trismegistus, Solomon and Socrates, Sibyls and Angels looked up at us from the pavement, and rows of popes kept watch from above the tall black and white pillars, while in the choir beyond priests chanted their solemn psalms. Next we were with the present in the gay Lizza, under the acacias and yellow chestnuts, by flower-beds full of roses and scarlet sage, and walls now covered with brilliant Virginia creepers; and out on the fort above to see a golden sky, and the sun disappearing behind banks of purple, golden-edged, and red clouds, and pale, misty hills; to look back across the gulf to the red town climbing up from low olive gardens towards the *Duomo* on its hill-top and tall La Mangia springing aloft from its own little hollow beyond. From every side came the voices of many people; of soldiers in the barracks, of women and children under the trees, of ball players in the old court below, and of applauding lookers-on lounging on the marble benches.

The tall unfinished arch of the *Duomo* that rises above houses and churches, and indeed above everything but the lofty La Mangia and the *Campanile*, tells the story of greatness and power and wealth suddenly checked. But the deadly plague, which carried off so many citizens that not even enough were left to make their city beautiful as they meant she should be, could not take away the beauty that was already hers nor kill the joyousness of her people.

There are no Spendthrift Clubs in Siena now, nor any gay Lanos, like him Dante met in the *Inferno*. But there are still laughter and song-loving Sienese, who, in their own simple fashion, go through life gathering rosebuds while they may. It seemed to us a very pretty fashion when we saw them holiday making on Sunday afternoon, peasants, priests, officers, townspeople, all out in their Sunday best, and

By the River.

when on the Via Cavour, near the *loggia*, we met two wandering minstrels singing love-songs through the town. One played on a mandoline which hung from his neck by a wide red ribbon, and as he played he sang. His voice was loud and strong and very sweet, and like another Orpheus he drew after him all who heard his music. His companion sold copies of the song, printed on pink paper, gay as the words. He went, bowing and smiling, in and out of the crowd; from the women, whose broad hats waved as they kept time to the singing, to the men who had stuck feathers in their soft felts, worn jauntily on one side, from demure little girls holding their nurses' hands to swaggering soldiers. Then when the first singer rested, he, in his turn, sang a verse. There was with them a small boy who every now and then broke in in a high treble, so that there was no pause in the singing.

Wherever we went that afternoon, whether

by the *Duomo* or out by the Porta Romana, on the Lizza or near San Domenico, we saw large written posters, announcing that at six in the evening there would be, at No. 17, Via Ricasoli, a great marionette performance of the *Ponte dei Sospiri.* Apparently this was to be the event of the day, and to it we determined to go. When a little before the appointed hour we came to the Via Ricasoli, we half expected to see a theatre ablaze with light. What we did find, after much difficulty, was low doorway on the ground floor of a many-storied palace, and before it a woman by a table, lighting a very small lamp, to the evident satisfaction of half a dozen youngsters. Over the open doorway was a chintz curtain. Behind it, darkness. This was not encouraging. But presently a woman with a child came to buy tickets. One of the group of youthful admirers was then sent up, and a second down, the street, and after they had come back with mysterious bundles, another lamp was produced, lit, and carried inside, and the first two of the audience followed. It was now within five minutes of six, so we also bought our tickets, three *soldi*, or cents, for each, and the curtain was drawn for us. A low, crypt-like room with vaulted ceiling; at one end two screens covered with white sheets; between them a stage somewhat larger than that of a street Punch, with a curtain representing a characteristic Sienese brick wall inclosing a fountain; several rows of rough wooden benches, and one of chairs — this was what we saw by the dim light of one lamp. We sat on the last bench. The audience probably would be more entertaining than the play. But the humble shall be exalted. The woman on the front row bade us come up higher. The small boy, who acted as usher told us we might have two of the chairs for two *soldi* more. The ticket-seller even came in, and in soft, pleading tones said that we might have any places we wanted; why then should we choose the worst? But we refused the exaltation.

The audience now began to arrive in good earnest. Five ragged boys of the *gamin* species, one of a neater order with his little sister by the hand, two soldiers, a lady with a blue feather in her bonnet and her child and nurse, two young girls, and the benches were almost filled. Our friend the ticket-seller became very active as business grew brisk. She was always running in and out, now giving this one a seat, now rearranging the reserved chairs, and now keeping the younger members of the audience in order. Her manner was gentle and insinuating. *Ragazzini*, she called the unruly boys who stood up on the benches and whistled and sang, so that I wondered what diminutive she gave the swells on the front row. This was amusing enough, but our dinner hour was half-past six. J—— looked at his watch. It was a quarter past. The ever-watchful keeper of the show saw him. "Ah! the *Signore* must not be impatient. *Ecco!* the music was about to begin." Begin it did indeed, to be continued with a persistency which made us fear it would never end. The musicians were two. A young man in a velveteen coat and long yellow necktie played the clarionet and another the cornet. They only knew one tune—a waltz, I think it was meant to be—but that they gave without stint, playing it over and over again, even while the ticket-seller made them move from their chairs, to a long high box by the wall; and when a third arrived with a trombone they let him join in when and as it best pleased him. When we had heard at least the twenty-fifth repetition of the waltz; had looked at the scuffling of the *ragazzini* until even that pleasure palled; had seen the soldiers smoke *cigaro Cavour* after *cigaro Cavour* so that the air grew heavy; and had watched the gradual growth of the audience until every place was filled, our patience was exhausted. Behold!

we said to the woman with the gentle voice, it was now seven. The play was announced for six. Was this right? In a house not far off every one was eating, and two covers were laid for us. But here we were in this dark room in our hunger, waiting for marionettes whose wires for aught we knew were broken! She became penitent. The *Signorini* must forgive her. The wires were not broken, but he who pulled them had not come. There was yet time. Would we not go and dine and then come back? She would admit us on our return.

And so we went and had our dinner, well seasoned with polite conversation. The ticket agent was true to her word. When we reappeared at her door, the curtain was pulled at once. In the meantime the musicians had been suppressed, not only out of hearing but out of sight. The room was so crowded that many who had arrived during our absence were standing. Indeed, by this time, there must have been at least five francs in the house. All were watching with entranced eyes the movements of four or five puppets. The scene represented an interior which, I suppose, was that of the prison on one side of the Bridge of Sighs. That it was intended for a cell also seemed evident, because the one portable piece of furniture on the stage was a low flat couch of a shape which, as every one who has been to the theatre, but never to prison, knows, is peculiar to the latter. It was impossible to lose sight of it, as the *dramatis personæ* made their exits and entrances over it. It was rather funny to see the villain of the piece after an outbreak of passion, or an elegant long-haired page in crimson clad, after a gentlemanly speech, suddenly vault over it. We could not discover what the play was about. Besides the two above-mentioned characters, there was a puppet with a large red face and green coat and trousers who gave moral tone to the dialogue, and another with heavy black beard and turban-like headdress, and much velvet and lace, whom we took to be a person of rank. As they came in and out by turn, it was impossible to decide which was the prisoner. With the exception of the jumps over the couch, there was little action in the performance. Its only two noticeable features were: first, the fact that villain, page, moralist, and magnate spoke in exactly the same voice and with the same expression; and, secondly, that they had an irrepressible tendency to stand in the air rather than on the floor, as if they had borrowed Mr. Stockton's negative gravity machine. The applause and laughter and rapt attention of the audience proved the play to be much to their liking. But for us inappreciative foreigners a little of it went a great way. As nothing but talk came of all the villainy and moralising and grandeur and prettiness—which may have been a clever bit of realism of which the English drama is not yet capable—and as there was no apparent reason why the dialogue should ever come to an end, we went away after the next act. The ticket-seller was surprised at our sudden change from eagerness to indifference, but not offended. She thanked us for our patronage, and wished us a *felice notte.*

With the darkness the gaiety of the town had increased. In the large theatre a play was being performed by a company of amateurs. Having had tickets given us, we looked in for a few minutes, but found it as wordy as that of the puppets. In a neighbouring *piazza* the proprietor of a large van, much like those to be seen in country fairs at home, was exhibiting a man, arrayed in a suit of rubber with a large brass helmet-like arrangement on his head, who, it seemed, could live at the bottom of the sea, along with Neptune and the Naiads, as comfortably as on dry shore. *Ecco!* There was the tank within where this marvel could be seen — a human being living under the water, and none the worse for it! Admission was four *soldi*, but *per militari e ragazzi*—for military and children—it was but two! So it seems that the soldiers, who abroad are to strike terror into the enemy, at home are ranked with the young of the land, since like them their name is legion! There were about a dozen in the crowd, and, all unconscious of the sarcasm, they hurried up the steps and into the show, while an old man ground out of a hand-organ the appropriate tune of *O que j'aime les militaires.*

But dramas and shows were not the only Sunday evening amusements. The *caffè* were crowded. Judging from the glimpses we had into little black cavern-like wine-shops, another Saint Bernardino is needed to set makers of gaming tools in Siena to the manufacture of holier articles. And more than once, as we walked homewards in the starlight, we heard the voices of three minstrels singing of human passion in the streets where Catherine so often preached the rapture of divine love. If swans were now seen in visions by fond Sienese matrons, they would wing their way earthward, and not heavenward as in the days when Blessed Bernardo's mother dreamed dreams.

AN ITALIAN BY-ROAD.

WE left Siena the morning after the Marionette Exhibition. The Major when he heard at breakfast that we were going, asked us point blank several questions about Boston publishers, his book probably being still uppermost in his thoughts. Later he sent his card to our room to know at what hour we started. He wished to see us off. The young lady of architectural proclivities shook hands and bade us good-bye, saying she had often ridden a sociable with her cousin in England.

After all there was not much for the Major to see. We could not ride through the streets, and so could not mount the machine for his benefit. But he was interested in watching us strap the bags to the luggage carrier, and pleased because of this opportunity to entertain us with more American reminiscences. I am afraid his amusement in Siena was small. In return for the little we gave him he asked us to come and see him in Rome, where he would spend the winter, and added that if we expected to pass through Cortona he would like to write a card of introduction for us to a friend of his there, an Italian who had married an English lady. Cortona was a rough place; and we might be glad to have it. He had forgotten his friend's name, but he would run up stairs and his wife could tell him. In a minute he returned with the written card. We have had many letters of introduction, but never one as singular as the Major-general's. As he knew our name even less well than that of his Cortona friend's, he introduced us as an "American lady and gentleman riding a *bicycle!*" Only fancy! as the English say. Our parting with him was friendly. Then he stood with Luigi and Zara until we disappeared round the corner of the street.

What a ride we had from Siena to Buonconvento! This time the road was all *giù, giù, giù.* It was one long coast almost all the way, and we made the most of it. We flew by milestone after milestone. Once we timed ourselves: we made a mile in four minutes. The country through which we rode was sad and desolate. On each side were low, rolling hills, bare as the English moors, and of every shade of grey and brown and purple. Here rose a hill steeper than the others, with a black cross on its summit; and here, one crowned with a group of four grim cypresses. Down the hillsides were deep ruts and gullies, with only an occasional patch of green, where women were watching sheep and swine. Once we came to three or four houses gathered round a small church, but they were as desolate as the land. We heard voices in the distance, but there was no one in sight.

When on a short stretch of level road we stopped to look at this strange grey land, the greyer because dark clouds covered the sky, we saw that above the barrenness the sun shone on Siena, and that all her houses, overtowered by the graceful La Mangia and the tall *Duomo Campanile*, glistened in the bright light.

About five miles from the city the desolation was somewhat relieved, for there were hedges by the roadside, and beyond, sloping olive-gardens and vineyards. Poplars grew by little streams, and sometimes we rode under oaks. On the top of every grey hill, giving it colour, was a farmhouse, rows of brilliant pumpkins laid on its red walls, ears of yellow corn hung in its *loggia*, and gigantic haystacks standing close by. There were monasteries too, great square brick buildings with tall towers, and below, spire-like cypresses. But between the farms and fertile fields were deep ravines and dry beds of streams. The road was lonely. Now and then flocks of birds flew down in front of the tricycle, or large white geese came out from under the hedge and hissed at us. For a few minutes a man driving a donkey-cart made the way not a little lively. He did not see us until we wheeled by him. Then he jumped as if he had been shot. "*Dio!*" he exclaimed, " but you frightened me!" He laughed, however, and whipping up his donkey rattled after us as if eager for a race, talking and shouting all the while and, until we were out of hearing. One or two peasants passed in straw, chariot-shaped wagons, and once from a farmhouse a woman in red blouse and yellow apron, with a basket on her head and a dog at her heels, came towards us. It was at this same farmhouse we met a Didymus. We stopped as we had a way of doing when anything pleased us; and he came out to have a better look at the *tramvai*. And how far did we expect to go to-day? he asked. To Monte Oliveto, J——

told him, for, like pious pilgrims, we thought to make a day's retreat with the monks there. "To Monte Oliveto! and in a day, and on that machine!" and he laughed us to scorn. "In a week, the *Signore* had better say." Later a stone-breaker's belief in us made some amends for the farmer's contempt. We were riding then. "*Addio!*" he cried, even before we reached him.

I shall always remember a little village through which we rode that morning because it was there we saw the first large stone-pine growing by the roadside which showed we were getting further south, and because of the friendliness of a peasant. It was a poor place. The people were ragged and squalid and sickly as if the gloom of the hills had fallen upon them. We asked at a shop for a lemon, but there was not one to be had. "Wait," cried a woman standing close by and she disappeared. She returned almost immediately with a lemon, on whose stem there were still fresh green leaves. "*Ecco!*" she said, "it is from my garden." "How much?" asked J—— as she handed it to him. "Oh, nothing, sir," and she put her hands behind her back. We made her take a few coppers, for the children, we told her. As far as it lay in her power, I think she was as courteous as those men in a certain Italian town, who, in days long past, fought together for the stranger who came within their gates, so eager were they all not to cheat him, as is the way with modern landlords, but to lodge him at their own expense, so that there were no inns in that town.

Before we reached Buonconvento the clouds rolled away and the sun came out. It had rained here earlier in the morning. The roads were sticky and the machine ran heavily, and trees and hedges were wet with sparkling raindrops. There is an imposing entrance to the little town—a pointed bridge over a narrow stream, with a Madonna and Child in marble relief at the highest point, an avenue of tall poplars with marble benches set between, and then the heavy brick walls, blackened with age, and the gateway, its high Gothic arch decorated with the old Sienese wolf, and a more recent crop of weeds.

We rode from one end to the other—a two minutes' ride — without finding a *trattoria*. At length we appealed to the crowd. Where was the *trattoria?* No one understood, and yet that very morning J—— had been asked if he were not a Florentine. "Perhaps *Monsieur* speaks French?" and a little Frenchman in seedy clothes jauntily worn, and with an indescribable swagger, came forward, hat in hand. The effect of his coming was magical. For unknown reasons, when it was found that J—— could speak French after a fashion, his Italian was all-sufficient. The *albergo* was here; we were directly in front of it, and the *padrone*, who had been at our elbows all the time, led the way into it. The Frenchman gallantly saw us through the crowd to the room where we were to dine. It was the best *trattoria* in the place, but poor enough, he said. Such bread and cheese! horrible! and he shrugged his shoulders and raised his hands to heaven in testimony thereof. He did not live in Buonconvento, not he. He came from Paris. Then he complimented J——— on his Italian, to make up in some measure for the failure of the people to appreciate it, and with a bow that might have won him favour at court, and a " I salute you, *Monsieur* and *Madame*," he politely left us before our dinner was served. He was a strolling actor, the *padrone* said; he and his troupe would give a performance in the evening.

The fact that we were going to Monte Oliveto annoyed the *padrone*. The monastery is a too successful rival to his inn. Few travellers except those who are on their way to Monte Oliveto pass through his town, and few who can help it stay there over night. His list of the evils we should have to endure was the sauce with which he served our beefsteak and potatoes. We must leave the post road for one that was stony and steep. Our *velocipede* could not be worked over it. It would take hours to reach the monastery, and we had better not be out after dark, for there were dangers untold by the way. But when he had said the worst he became cheerful, and even seemed pleased when we admired his kitchen, where brass and copper pots and pans hung on the walls, and where in one corner was a large fireplace with comfortable seats inside and a pigeon-house underneath. But when we complimented him on the walls of his town, Bah! he exclaimed, of what use were they? They were half destroyed. They would be no defence in war times.

He was right. The walls, strong by the gate, have in parts entirely disappeared, and in others houses and stables have been made of them. It is on the open space by these houses that the men have their playground.

They were all there when we arrived, and still there when we left. Young men, others old enough to be their fathers, and boys were, each in turn, holding up balls to their noses, and then, with a long slide and a backward twist of the arm, rolling them along the ground, which is the way Italians play bowls.

Before the afternoon was over we cursed in our hearts the Tuscan politeness we had heretofore praised. About a mile from Buonconvento the road to Monte Oliveto divided. We turned to the right. But two peasants with ox-teams called out from below that we must not go that way. It was all bad. But to the left it was good, and *piano*, ascending but gently, and we had much better take it. In an evil moment we did. That it ill behoves a wise man to seek counsel in every word spoken to him we found to our cost. In the first place the ascent was not gentle; we had not then learned that an Italian calls every hill that is not as straight up and down as the side of a house, *piano*. And in the second place the road was not good, but vilely bad. Unfortunately for half a mile, or perhaps more, it was fair enough. But when we had gone just so far that we were unwilling to turn back, we discovered our mistake. The road we had not taken was that built by the monks hundreds of years ago; we had chosen the new and not yet finished by-way. It was heavy with dust and dirt, and full of ruts and loose stones. Over it we could not ride or even push the tricycle without difficulty. It was in keeping, however, with the abomination of desolation lying on each side. For we were now in a veritable wilderness, a land of deserts and of pits where few men dwelt. All around us were naked, colourless chalk hills, abrupt precipices and ravines. A few chestnut trees, a rose bush covered with red berries growing from the grey earth were the only green things we passed for miles. It was weary and slow work, and the sun was low on the hill-tops before we came to the point where the two roads met. At some distance above us we saw a large red building surrounded by cypresses, and we knew this must be Monte Oliveto Maggiore. So we took heart again.

But our trouble was not over. The road was better only by comparison, and it was still impossible to ride, and hard work to push or pull the tricycle. It was made of bricks which lay as if they had been carelessly shot out of a cart and left where and when they fell. A little further on it divided again. A woman was walking towards us, and J—— asked her which was the road to the convent —*il convento?* "You must go back," she said, "it lies miles below, Buonconvento." "These peasants are fools," said J—— in angry English to her very face, but she, all unconscious, smiled upon us. We went to the left, which fortunately was just what we ought to have done. But it was provoking that, instead of getting

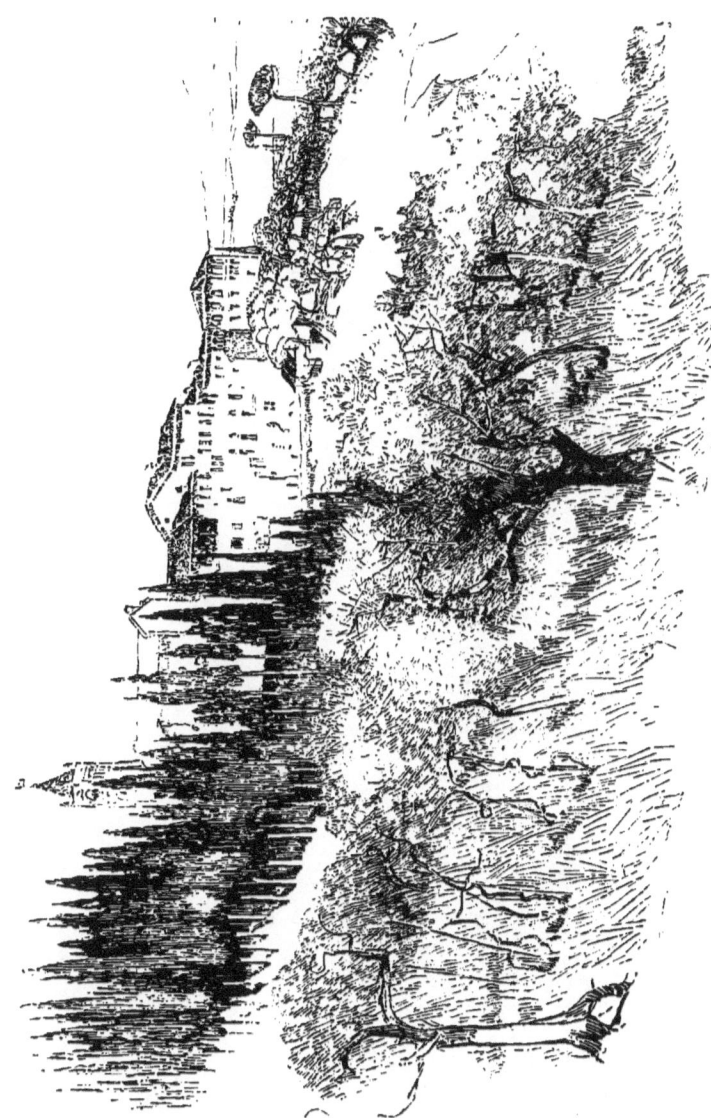

Monte Oliveto.

nearer to the monastery we seemed to be going farther from it. With one turn of the road it appeared to be above, and with the next below us. Now it was on one side and now on the other, until I began to feel as if we were the answer to the riddle I had so often been asked in my childhood, the mysterious "What is it that goes round and round the house but never gets in?" Soon the sun set behind the hills, and the sky grew soft and roseate. We met several peasants bearing large fagots of twigs on their heads. There were one or two shrines, a chapel, and a farm-house, in front of which a priest stood talking to a woman. But on we went without resting, J—— pushing the machine and I walking behind, womanlike, shirking my share of the work. The road grew worse until it became nothing but a mass of ruts and gullies washed out by the rain, and led to a hill from which even Christian would have turned and fled. But we struggled up, reaching the top to see the gate of the monastery some sixty or seventy feet below. Finally we came to the great brick gateway which in the dull light, for by this time the colour had faded from the sky, rose before us a heavy black pile, beyond whose archway we saw only shadow and mystery. As we walked under it, our voices when we spoke were unnatural and hollow. On the other side the road wound through a gloomy grove of cypresses, growing so close together that they hedged us about with impenetrable darkness. Once several silent figures, moving noiselessly, passed by. Had we, by mischance, wandered into a Valley of the Shadow of Death?

The cypress grove, after several windings, brought us face to face with the building at which we had already so often looked from the distance. Even in the semi-darkness we could see the outline distinctly enough to know we were standing in front of the church, and that the detached building a little to our left was a barn or stable. But not a light shone in a window, not a doorway was in sight. I recalled my convent experience of bygone years, and remembered that after eight o'clock in the evening no one was admitted within its walls. Was there a rule like this at Monte Oliveto, and was six the hour when its bolts and bars were fastened against the stranger? As we hesitated where to go or what to do next, three or four workmen came from the stable. J—— spoke to them, and one offered to show him the entrance to the monastery while I waited by the tricycle. It was strange to stand in the late evening and in the wilderness alone with men whose speech I barely understood and whose faces I could not see. For fully five minutes I waited thus while they talked together in low voices. But at last I heard one cry. *Ecco!* here was the *padrone;* and they all took off their hats. A dog ran up and examined me, and then a man, who I could just make out in the gloom wore a cassock and the broad-brimmed priestly hat, joined the group. "*Buona sera*," he said to me. "Could I speak to him in French?" I asked. "Yes," he assented. "What was it I wanted?" When I told him we wished to stay in the monastery, he said he had not expected us. We had not written.

"But," I exclaimed, "we thought strangers were allowed to stay here."

"Yes," he answered; "there is a *pension* in the monastery; but it is for artists."

"And my husband is an artist," I interrupted eagerly, for from his manner I feared he would refuse us admission. After all, what did he know about us, except that, vagrant-like, we were wandering in the mountains at a most unseasonable hour? Indeed, when later I reflected on the situation, I realised that we must have seemed suspicious characters. At this critical moment J—— returned. His guide had led him to a small side door beyond the church. There he had rung and rung again. The bell was loud and clear and roused many echoes within, but nothing else. The guide, perplexed, then led him back. I told him with whom I was speaking, and he continued the conversation with the *padrone*. Had they talked in Italian only or in French, they might have understood each other; but instead they used a strange mixture of the two, to their mutual bewilderment. If this kept on much longer we should undoubtedly spend the night in the open air. In despair I broke in, in French, " But, father, cannot we stay this one night ? "

"Certainly," he said, fortunately dropping all Italian. "That is what I was explaining to *Monsieur*. You can stay, but of course we have nothing prepared. We will do our best."

If he had said he would do his worst, provided we were rid of the tricycle for the night, and were ourselves indoors where we might sit down, we should have been thankful.

The bags were unstrapped and given into the care of one of the men, a place was made for the machine in the stable, and then we followed the *padrone* or *Abate*—for this was his real title—to the door where J—— had rung in vain, and which he opened with his key. Within it was so dark that we groped our way through the hall and a small cloister. Then we came to a flight of steps where, at the bidding of the *Abate*, as if to reassure us that we were not being led to secret cells or torture chambers, the man carrying our bags struck a solitary match. By this feeble light we walked up the broad stone stairs, and through many passage-ways, not a sound breaking the stillness but our steps and their loud echoes, to a door where the *Abate* left us, and at the same time the match burnt out. But the next minute he reappeared with a lighted taper, and at the end of the hall opened another door, lit a lamp on a table within, and showed us four rooms, which, he said, were at our disposal. The beds were not made, but they would be attended to immediately. He had now to say Office, but at nine supper would be served. Here was a very comfortable solution to the mystery into which the massive gateway seemed to lead. The Valley of the Shadow of Death had turned out to be a Delectable Land.

It was still more comfortable later, when, his Office said, the *Abate* came back and sat and talked with us. Now he could examine us by a better light, I think he concluded we were not dangerous characters, probably only harmless lunatics. However that may be, after half an hour when the supper-bell rang, and we started off for the refectory, again by the light of his taper, we were the best of friends. The long corridor, thus dimly seen, seemed interminable. We went down one staircase, to find the door locked against us, then up and down another. Here the light went out, leaving us in a darkness like unto that of Egypt. The *Abate* laughed as if it was the best of jokes. He took J——'s hand and J—— took mine, and thus like three children we went laughing down the staircase, and along more passages, and at last into a long refectory, at the further end of which was a lamp, while a door, to one side of that by which we entered, opened, and a second monk in white robes, holding a lighted taper, came in, and when he saw us made a low bow. As there were no other visitors, we were to eat with him and his brother monk, the *Abate* said; and then he gave me the head of the table, asking me if I were willing to be the Lady Abbess.

If we had been two prodigals, he could not have been kinder than he was, now he had given us shelter. If we had been starving like the hero of the parable, he could not have been more anxious to set before us a feast of plenty. Nor would any fatted calf have been more to our taste than the substantial supper prepared for us. We must eat, he said. We needed it. He had seen us coming up the hill as he talked with a peasant by the roadside. But *Monsieur* was push-pushing the machine and looking at nothing else, and *Madame* was panting and swinging her arms, staring straight in front of her; and before he had time to speak we had passed. We must drink too. The wine was good for us. We must not mix water with it. It was Christian; why then should it be baptised? The White Brother spoke little, but he never allowed J——'s plate to remain empty. When the meat was brought in we were joined by Pirro, a good sized dog with no tail to speak of, and Lupo, an unusually large cat, and his numerous family, who all had to be fed at intervals.

But even while Pirro jumped nimbly into the air after pieces of bread thrown to him, and Lupo scratched, and his progeny made mournful appeals to be remembered, and we talked, I looked every now and then down the long, narrow table to where it was lost in deep shadow. The cloth was laid its entire length, as if in readiness for the banished brothers whenever they might return. I should not have been surprised then to see the door open to admit a procession of white monks, all with tapers in their hands. The *Abate* must have realised that to a stranger there was something uncanny in his dark, silent, deserted monastery, and his last word as he bade us good-night was that we were to fear nothing, but to sleep in peace.

MONTE OLIVETO.

THE days we spent at Monte Oliveto were golden days. For we not only slept there one, but several nights, and the *Abate* declared we could remain as long as we might care to. Nothing could be more melancholy and wild than the country into which we had come. It is the most desolate part of all that strange desolation which lies to the south-east of Siena. The mountain on which the monastery is built is surrounded on every side but one by deep, abrupt ravines. Behind it rise higher mountains, bare and bleak and grey, like gigantic ash-piles, and on the very highest peak is the wretched little village of Chiusure. The other hills around are lower, and from the road by the convent gateway one can see Siena, pale and blue on the horizon, and southward, over the barren hill-tops, Monte Amiata. But Monte Oliveto with its gardens and orchards and vineyards, is a green place in the midst of the barrenness. The mountain sides are terraced, and olives and vines grow almost to the bottom of the ravine. It was said in old times that the Bishop of Arezzo was commanded in a vision to call the monastery after the Mount in Jerusalem. Nowadays sceptics say the trees on the terraces explain the name, forgetting that in the beginning this hill was as bare as the others. Why cannot it be believed for the legend's sake that the olives were planted afterwards because of the name?

The first morning the *Abate* took us to see the frescoes representing the life of St. Benedict, painted on the walls of the large cloister. I will be honest, and confess that they disappointed us. I doubt whether the artists were very proud of them. Luca Signorelli,

Chiusure.

before he had finished the first side of the cloister, gave up the work, as it is not likely he would have done had he cared much for it. Sodoma, when he took his place, was at first so careless that the then abbot took him to task, but the artist calmly told him more could not be expected for the price that was paid him. Certainly with neither were these frescoes a labour of love, and this one feels at once. One wonders if this could have been the same Sodoma who painted the St. Sebastian in Florence, and yet there is more charm in his pictures than in those of Signorelli. But what I cared for most were his portraits of himself, with heavy hair hanging about his face, and wearing the cloak the Milanese gentleman, turned monk, had given him, and of his wife and child; and the pictures of the raven and the other pets he brought with him to the monastery, to the wonder of the good monks.

It is a pity every one cannot look at these frescoes with such loving, reverential eyes as the *Abate*. He had shown them probably to hundreds of visitors; he had seen them almost every day for the many years he had been at Monte Oliveto; but his pleasure in them was as fresh as if it dated but from yesterday. He told the story of each in turn—of how in this one the great St. Benedict put the devil to flight, and how in that he, by a miracle, recalled an erring brother; and once he pointed to a palm-tree in a background. Sodoma, he said, had seen and admired a palm in the garden of the monastery, and so, after his realistic fashion, had painted it in just as he had his pets. That very tree was in the garden still. He would show it to us if we liked.

There never was such another garden! It is close to the large brick house or palace by the gateway, where in old times lay visitors were lodged, and beyond which no woman was ever allowed to pass. It is small, but in it the monks only raised the rarest trees and plants. Here grew the precious herbs out of which in the pharmacy, whose windows overlooked the quiet green inclosure, they prepared the healing draughts for which people came from far and near. The pharmacy is closed now. There is dust in the corners and on the quaint old chairs. Cobwebs hang from the ceiling. But brass scales are still on the heavy wooden counter, and pestle and mortar behind it, and glass retorts of strange shapes in the corners and above the doors. Majolica jars, all marked with the three mountains, the cross and olive-branch, the *stemma* of the monastic order, are ranged on the brown shelves, many of the large ones carefully sealed, while from the smaller come forth strange odours of myrrh and incense and rare ointments. As in the refectory, everything here is in order for the monks when they return. But they will find more change in the garden below. The rare plants, the ebony and the hyssop, the cactuses and the palm, which made us think even less of Sodoma's frescoes than we had before, the pomegranates and the artichokes, are all there. But weeds grow in the paths, and by the old grey well, and in among the herbs; roses have run riot in the centre of the garden and turned it into a wild, tangled growth. To us it seemed the loveliest spot in Monte Oliveto. The hours spent in it were like a beautiful idyl of Theocritus or Shelley. The sun shone and the air was filled with sweet spicy scents. To one side was the grey mountain, to the other dense cypresses, and above a blue, cloudless sky. The roses were still in bloom, and as we lingered there the *Abate* went from bush to bush, and picked for me a large bunch of fragrant buds. I hope if the monks ever do come back, that, while they throw open the windows of the pharmacy and let the light in again upon the majolica and the dark wood-work, they will leave the gates of the garden locked. It is fairer in its confusion than it ever could be with weeded paths and well-clipped bushes.

The *Abate* took us everywhere—through

the empty guest-chambers of the palace to the tower, now a home for pigeons, from the top of which one has a wide view of the country, which, with its squares of olives and its grey hills and fields marked by deep furrows as if by boundary lines, looks like a large map or geological chart; through the monastery, with its three hundred rooms with now but three monks to occupy them; its cloisters, for there are two besides the large frescoed one; its *loggie*, where geraniums and other green plants were growing; its great refectory, beyond the door of which fowl or flesh meat never passed, and which is now used no longer; and its library, at the very top of the house, where rows of white vellum volumes are ready for the students who so seldom come. Then he led us to the church, where there are more altars than monks to pray before them, and a wonderful choir with inlaid stalls; and in and out of little chapels, one of which contains the grotto where blessed Bernardo Tolomei, the founder of the order, lived for many years after he came to the wilderness, while another was the first church used by the brotherhood, and the Virgin with angels playing to her on harps and mandolines, above the altar, was painted long before Signorelli and Sodoma began their work. Then there was the lemon-grove to be seen, where the *Abate* filled our pockets with the ripe fruit, which we were to keep, he said, in case we might be thirsty on the road some day when there was no wine or water near by to drink. And after that there was still to be visited the wine-press, with its deep shadows, and dark corners, and long subterranean passage to the room below, where men were filling small casks from large butts and then carrying them off on their shoulders to be weighed and stored above. We had to taste the wine, and I think it, together with the sunshine and the flowers, must have gone to our heads that morning and stayed there so long as we were at Monte

Oliveto, for everything about us seemed to belong less to the actual world than to a dreamland full of wonder and beauty and sometimes of pathos.

It was the same in the afternoon, when the *Abate* had gone about his work—for he is a busy man, like the centurion with many under him—and J—— and I wandered alone over the grey hills up to Chiusure. Life with its hardships must be real enough to the people of this little village, in which seeds of pestilence, sown hundreds of years ago, still bear the bitter fruit of wretchedness. It seems as if the brick walls which could not keep out the plague have ever since successfully barred the way to all prosperity, for generation after generation is born within them but to live and die in poverty. We saw melancholy figures there, old hags of women, with thin white hair and bent almost double under heavy bundles of wood, toiling up steep, stony streets with bare feet, and others crouching in the gloom opposite open doorways. Even the little priest, who, in his knee-breeches and long frock-coat and braided smoking-cap with tassels dangling in his eyes, humorous enough to look at, was pathetic in his way. For, after he had shown us his church with its decorations, poor as the people who worship in it, and offered us a glass of wine in his own parlour, he spread on the table before us some broken pieces of glass easily put together, on which a picture was painted. Was it of value? he asked, so eagerly that he told without further words the story of wants but ill supplied. He was willing to sell it, but he did not know what it was worth. Could we tell him? No, we could not, we said, for we really knew nothing about it, though we feared the hopes he had set upon it would never be realised. And then sadly he gathered together the pieces and put them away again in their newspaper wrapping.

It was more cheerful outside the gateway.

There, in the late afternoon, the grey olives by the way were more clearly defined against the sky, and the grey ravines below more indistinct. Beyond, the hills, now all purple and soft, rolled away to the horizon and to the brilliant red sky above. One or two lights were lit in distant farm-houses, and once we heard a far-off bell. Before us the white road led by one green hill on whose top was a circle of cypresses, and in its centre a black cross, as in so many old pictures.

But the strangest part of this dream-life was the friendship that sprang up between us and the monks. I should not have been more surprised if St. Benedict and Blessed Bernardo had come back to earth to make friends with us. It was not only that the *Abate* acted as our guide through the monastery. This he does for every visitor who comes, since the Government took possession of it and turned it into a public art gallery and *pension* for artists. But he came to our room early in the morning to drink his coffee with us, and in the evening, after he had said his Office, for a little talk. And when we had finished our supper we sat together long over our wine, talking now in French, now in English, now in Italian, and occasionally understanding each other. Like all good fellows, we too had our jokes. But the *Abate's* favourite was to tell how he had seen us coming up the mountain, *Monsieur* push-pushing the *velocipede* and *Madame* puff-puffing behind him. Even Dom Giuseppe, the other monk—the third was away—relaxed from the dignity with which he had first met us, and took part in the talk and the laughter. Unreal as seemed these late suppers in the long refectory, in the dim light, with Pirro for ever jumping after choice morsels while Lupo and his family growled with rage and envy from under the table, we strayed even farther into Wonderland the second day after our arrival, when both monks went out for a ride on the tricycle along the mulberry walk and by Blessed Bernardo's grotto.

The last day of our stay a number of visitors arrived—a priest from Perugia, two nuns, and two English ladies. They were not expected, and dinner had to be prepared for them. The *Abate* is never pleased when guests come without giving him warning. When we met him in the refectory a little after twelve, we could see his patience had been tried. We must pardon him for being late, he said, but he had had to find something to eat for all these people. Were they to dine with us? we asked. No, indeed, was his answer. They were not members of the community. This confirmed our doubts as to whether we might not be monks without our knowing it; for the first morning the *Abate* had given us a key of the great front door, by which we could let ourselves in at all hours, without any ringing of bells or calling of porters, so that we felt as if we belonged to the convent. These visitors were the thorns in his present life, the *Abate* continued, and we were his roses. Then he brought out a bottle of the *vino santo* which he makes himself, and prizes so highly that he never sells it as he does the other wines, and a plate of grapes for which he had sent a great distance. And when dinner was over he bade the servant put all that was left of grapes and wine away. They were for the community, and not for common folk. He introduced us to the Perugian priest, who might possibly, he said, be of use to us in Perugia. The latter almost embraced J—— in his protestations of goodwill, and came running back several times to press his hand, and say in a French of his own invention that we must call often during our stay in his city.

THROUGH THE WILDERNESS TO A GARDEN.

WE left the monastery the next morning. It took courage on our part. But we knew it was best to go quickly. Every day we fell more under the dreamy influence of the place and became less willing for action. We must hasten from Monte Oliveto, for the very reason which led Blessed Bernardo to it—to flee temptation. The *Abate* was in our room by half-past seven. Dom Giuseppe was in the church saying mass, but had sent his farewells. He himself had not yet said mass, so he could not drink his coffee with us, but he sat by while we had ours. We should not reach San Quirico till noon, he feared, and we must have something in our pockets to eat in the meantime, and he went to his room and came back with two cakes. He brought besides two letters he had written introducing us to monks at San Pietro in Perugia. Then he came down stairs and out to the stable, though he was fasting, and the morning was wet and cloudy and cold. We did not get on the tricycle at once. We remembered the road too well. The *Abate* walked by our side, now and then patting J——on the back and calling him affectionately "Giuseppe, Giuseppe," and kept with us until, at some little distance from the gateway, we mounted the machine. After he had said good-bye he stood quietly watching us. Then there came a turn in the road which hid him from us, and when we saw him again he was walking on the foot-path below the cypresses, with two little boys who had come out with him. He was on his way to take Dom Giuseppe's place at the altar. And then we went on sadly, for we knew that we should not come to another resting-place where there was such perfect relief for pilgrims that are weary and faint in the way.

As the road was difficult going up, so was it dangerous coming down, and again we had to walk. To add to our discomfort, before long it began to rain, and it was so cold we had to blow on our fingers to keep them warm. During the night it had snowed on the far mountain ranges. Beyond Buoncon vento, when we returned to the post-road, we went fast enough, but only for a while. There were more mountains to cross, up which J—— could not go very fast because of the burden, or knapsack, that was on his back. Out of very shame I took my share in pushing and pulling the tricycle. Once or twice we had long coasts; but in places the road was sandy, and in descending wound as often as a small St. Gothard Railway. Coasting would have been too great a risk, especially as I never could begin back-pedalling going down hill, though on up-grades but too often, J—— complained, that like Dante on the hill-side my firm foot ever was the lower! The way still lay between and over hills of chalk, and we rode for miles through monotonous barrenness. It rained at intervals, but at times the sun almost broke through the clouds which followed it in long grey sweeps from the white masses on the snow-capped mountains bounding the horizon. To our right, Monte Amiata, bare and rugged and with white top, was always in sight, and once, above it, the clouds rolled away, leaving a broad stretch of greenish-blue sky. There were many crosses by the wayside, and they were different from any we had yet seen. On each, above spear and sponge, was a black cock, rudely carved to look as if it were crowing. Just before we came to San Quirico, and towards noon, we saw at the foot of one of these crosses an old, weary-looking peasant, with head bowed, as if he listened for the Angelus.

We were prepossessed against San Quirico before we reached it. Olives with vines hanging from them, in defiance of Virgil, brown fields, and red and yellow trees could not reconcile us to the long climb up the mountain. It was worth our trouble, however, if only to see the cathedral. We left the tricycle at the *trattoria*, and at our leisure looked at the portal and its pillars, with quaintly carved capitals of animals and birds, and those others, joined together with a Celtic-like twist and resting on leopards, and the two sea-monsters above. And while we looked at the grotesque gargoyles on the walls, and the two figures for columns, and the lions on the side doorway, two *carabinieri* from a neighbouring window examined us as if we were equal curiosities. This fine building is an incongruity in San Quirico, which—for our first impressions proved right—is at best but a poor place. We were cheated in it as we had never been before. When we went back to the *trattoria* four men were eating their dinner inside the fire-place in the kitchen. But we were ushered into what I suppose was the best room. It was dining-room and bed-chamber combined. On one side was a long table, on the other the bed. The dressing-table served as buffet, and the *padrona* brought from its drawers the cheese and apples for our dessert. In the garden below, for we were in the second story, weeds like corn grew so tall that they shaded the window. What happened in that room, and the difference that arose between the *padrona* and ourselves, are facts too unpleasant to recall! But I am sure the next foreigners who went to San Quirico heard doleful tales of the evil doings of the two *Inglesi* who came on a *velocipede*.

After San Quirico there was the same barrenness, and only indifferent roads over rolling country. Until within half a mile of Pienza, where the hedges began again, not a tree grew by the roadside, and the only signs of vegetation were the reeds in the little dark pools dotting the grey fields. It was still bitterly cold, and my fingers tingled on the handles. Once we passed a farmhouse where a solitary woman watched a herd of black swine, and once we met the diligence. That was all.

We rode into Pienza, though our way lay to one side of it. But we were curious to see the cathedral and palaces Pius II. built there, in the fond hope of turning his native village into an important town. Of all the follies of proud popes I think this was the greatest. As well might he have hoped by his single effort to cover the *creta*, or chalk, with roses as to raise a prosperous city in its midst. We saw the great brown buildings marked with the five crescents of the Piccolomini and the papal tiara and keys, as out of place in Pienza as the cathedral seemed in San Quirico; we looked closer at the old stone well and its beautiful wrought iron work. J—— made a sketch of a fine courtyard, and then we were on the road again.

Near Montepulciano we came to a thickly wooded country, riding for several miles between chestnuts and oaks. There were open places too, from which we saw far below the fair Val di Chiana, and in the distance Lake Thrasymene, pale and silvery; and close by olive gardens, through whose grey branches we looked at the purple mountains and their snowy summits. Above were broad spaces of bright sky, for the dark clouds were rolling away beyond the lake, and those that floated around Monte Amiata were now glistening and white. We had left the wilderness for a garden. All the bells rang out a welcome when, after working up the long road—so winding that at times the city was completely hidden—we wheeled into the now dark and cold streets of Montepulciano.

THE PILGRIMS ARE DETAINED IN MONTEPULCIANO.

It was in this high hill town that one of the pilgrims fell by the way. For two days J——— was too ill to ride, and we feared our pilgrimage had come to an end. We stayed at the Albergo Marzocco, whose praises Mr. Symonds has sung. It was on the fifth floor of an old palace, and the entrance was through the kitchen. The *padrone* and his family were very sociable. Almost immediately his wife wanted to know the trade of the *Signore*. "Ah! an artist. *Eccomi!* I am a washer-woman!" She was also cook. From the dining-room we could watch her as she prepared our meals. When she kept us waiting too long we had only to step into the kitchen and stand over her until the dish we had ordered was ready. We could look too into an adjacent room, where during our stay one daughter of the house for ever ironed table-cloths, while a second added up endless accounts.

But friendly as these people were, they were stupid. The *padrone* had a *pizzicheria*, or pork shop, across the street. When anything was wanted at the inn, it was brought from the shop. Every time I went to my window I saw messengers on their way between the two establishments. But no man can serve two masters. The *pizzicheria* drove a more thriving trade and the inn suffered in consequence. It was left in the charge of a youth of unparalleled stupidity, who seldom understood what we asked for, and when he did declared it something not to be had. But a friend was sent to us in our need.

It happened in this way. The first morning

we went out for a walk. As we started a harlequin, newly painted in red and white, struck nine from a house-top near by. In the Via dell' Erbe, women, their heads covered with gay handkerchiefs or wide-brimmed, high-crowned felt hats, were selling vegetables and fruit. Just in front of us were three beggars, two blind and one lame, walking hand in hand, and an old brown monk with a wine cask on his shoulder. At almost every turn we saw through an archway the three far away lakes of Montepulciano, Chiusi and Thrasymene. But it was now J—— began to feel ill, and we went into a *caffè* and called for cognac. As we sat there the door opened, and a young Italian dressed *à l'Anglaise*, even to his silver-headed cane, came in. He took a seat at the table next to us. When his coffee was brought in he asked the waiter if he had seen the English lady and gentleman who had arrived the evening before on a *velocipede*. No, the *cameriere* had not; he knew nothing of these *forestieri.* There was a pause while the young Italian sipped his coffee. But presently he turned to us and said in good English, but with a marked accent:

"I beg pardon, sare, but was it not you who came to Montepulciano on a tricycle?"

"Yes," J—— said, rather curtly.

"Ah, I thought so!" the Italian continued, well satisfied with the answer. "I have seen it—a Humber. It is a beautiful machine. I myself do ride a bicycle, the *Speecial Cloob.* You know it? I do belong to the *Cyclists' Touring Cloob,* and to the *Speedvell Cloob.* All the champions belong to that *Cloob.* I did propose some one for director at the last meeting; you will see my name on that account in the papers. Here is my card, but in the country around Montepulciano all call me Sandro or Sandrino. I have ridden from Florence to Montepulciano in one day. I have what you call the wheel-fever," and he smiled apologetically and stopped, but only to take breath.

We were fellow-cyclers and that was enough. We were friends at once, though J—— was too ill to be enthusiastic, and though our record would have disgusted the *Speedvell Cloob*. He was sorry J—— was not well. He could sympathise. He was feeling *vary bad* himself, because the day before he had gone on his bicycle as far as Montalcino with a gun to *keel the little birds*. It was too far even for a champion. But he had taken the waters—Janos—he had great faith in the waters. The cognac had by this time made J—— better, and we started to leave the *caffè*. Sandrino, to give him his Montepulciano name, insisted on paying for everything. We must let him have that favour, he said, and also another. He was not a native of the town. He was a Roman, as he supposed we could see by his nose. But still he would like to do us the honours of the place. He would take us to see so fine a church. We could not but be pleased with it. It was only a step. Foolishly we went. The step was a long one. It took us half way down the mountain-side to the Madonna di San Biagio. But J—— was now really too wretched to look at anything, and we turned back at once. As we walked slowly up again Sandrino explained that he had lived in England several years, and it turned out that he had the English as well as the wheel fever. All his clothes were from London, he said. He smoked English tobacco. A friend sent it to him, and he showed us the small paper box tied with a string in which he kept it. And most of his news was English, too. His friends wrote him. He had just had a letter—see—and he opened it. There had been fearful riots in England. He cared much for the politics of the country. But the refrain to all he said was praise of cycling. He offered to ride with us when we left Montepulciano. He could go any day but the next, which was his twenty-first birthday, and when he was to have a great dinner and many friends and much wine. He would call, if we would allow him, and with profession of great friendship he left us at the door of the inn.

He was true to his word. Indeed, I do not know what had become of us but for his kindness. We were both depressed by this unlooked-for delay, and he not only helped to amuse but was of practical use to us. He came twice the following day. The first time he stopped, he said, to tell us he did hear from friends in Castiglione del Lago, who, if we would ride to-morrow, would be glad to see us at lunch. " There will be nothing much," he concluded. " They will make no preparations. We just take whatever they have. It will be some *leetle* thing." Though in the first glory of his twenty-one years, he went with me to a druggist's to act as interpreter. But I think he was repaid by his pleasure in carrying back a bottle of his favourite waters. The *cameriere*, when he saw it, with his usual cleverness followed into the room with three glasses. If we had asked for three, he would have brought one. Sandrino's second visit was in the evening, after he had eaten his great dinner and drunk much wine, which had again made him feel *vary bad*. Had we ever tasted the famous Montepulciano, " king of all wine " ? he asked. No? Well, we must before leaving the town. It was not to be had in the shops. He had been presented with many bottles. He repeated his invitation to lunch in Castiglione, and it seemed that other friends in a villa near Cortona would also be charmed to see us, and to give us wine if we were tired.

IN THE VAL DI CHIANA.

THE next morning J—— was much better, and we decided to ride. Sandrino arrived at half-past seven and breakfasted with us. In the uniform of the *Speedvell Cloob*, its monogram in silver on his cap, he was even more English than he had been the day before. Our last experience at the *albergo* was characteristic. The *cameriere*, overcome by Sandrino's appearance, became incapable of action. We called for our coffee and rolls in vain. Finally, we all, our guest included, made a descent upon the kitchen and forced him to bestir himself.

It was Sunday morning, and the news of our going had been noised abroad. The aristocracy as well as the people turned out to see us off. Many of Sandrino's friends lingered in the barber's shop across the street. Others waited just without the city gate with his mother and sister. When Sandrino saw the crowd he sprang upon his *Speecial Cloob*, worked with one foot and waved the other in the air, rode to the little park beyond and back, and then jumped off, hat in hand, at his mother's side, with the complacent smile of a champion. Indeed, the whole ride that day savoured of the circus. He went down hills with his legs stretched straight out on either side. On level places he made circles and fancy figures in the road. Whenever we passed peasants—and there were many going to church—he shrieked a warning, shrill as a steam-engine whistle. No wonder he said he had no use for a bell! He spoke to all the women, calling them his " beautiful cousins." And in villages the noise he made was so great that frightened people, staring at him,

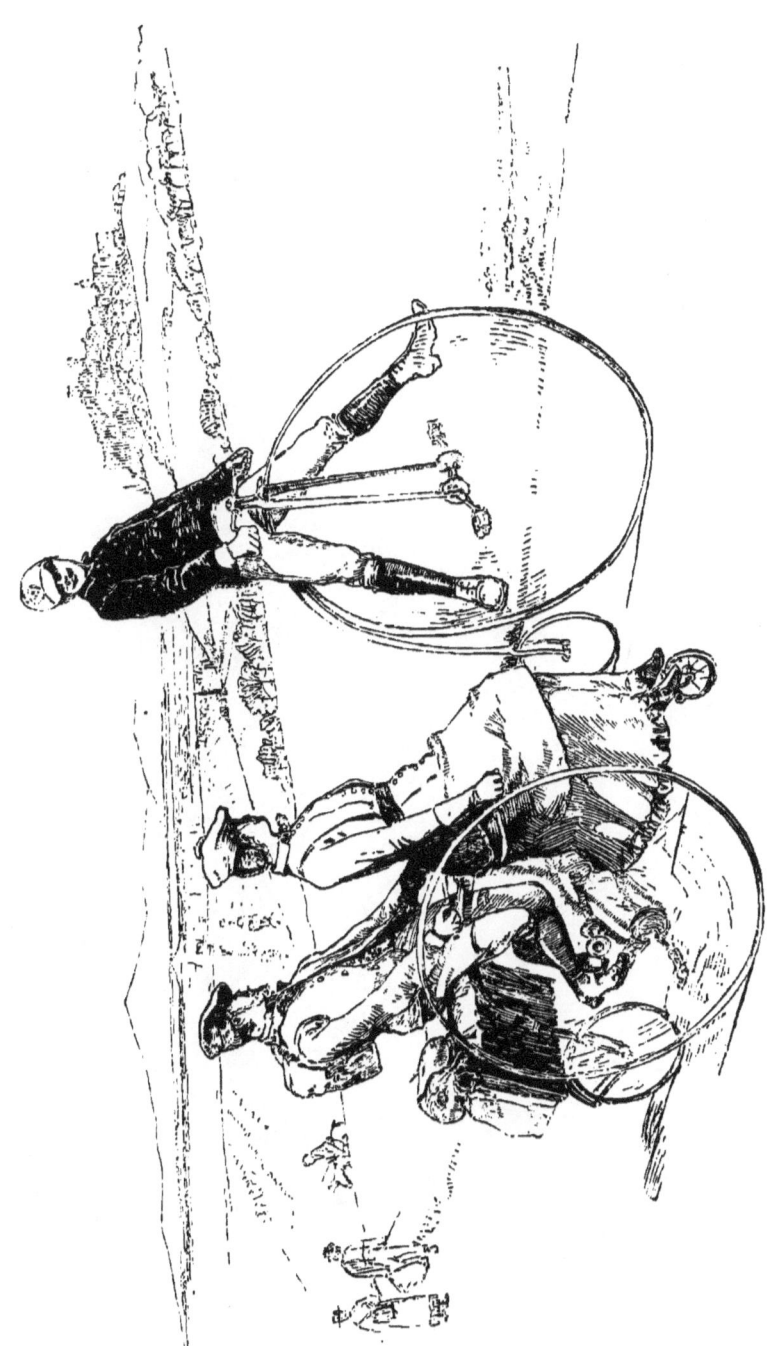
Leaving Montepulciano.

never looked behind, so that several times we all but rode over men and women who walked backward right into our wheels. And all the while J——, like the ring-master, kept calling and shrieking, but no one paid the least attention to him.

Our way was through the beautiful Val di Chiana, no longer pestilential and full of stenches as in Dante's day, but fresh and fair, and in places sweet with clematis. There were no fences or hedges, and it stretched from mountains to mountains, one wide lovely park. About half way to Castiglione we came to the boundary line between Tuscany and Umbria, a canal with tall poplars on its banks, throwing long reflections into the water below, where a boat lay by the reeds. We stopped there some little time. Sandrino was polite, but I could see he did not approve. What would the *Speedvell Cloob* have thought? Farther on, when we loitered again, near a low farmhouse under the oaks, he wheeled quickly on. But presently he came back. "Oh," he said, "I thought you must have had an accident!"

There could be no lovelier lake town than Castiglione del Lago. The high hill on which it stands projects far into Lake Thrasymene. The olives, which grow from its walls down the hill-side into the very water, are larger and finer with more strangely twisted trunks than any I have ever seen. As we came near the town we rode between them, looking beneath their silvery-grey branches out to the pale blue quiet lake beyond. A woman came from under their shade with a bundle of long reeds on her head. A priest passed us on a donkey.

We left our machines in a stable at the foot of the hill, and walked through the streets. Here Sandrino's invitation came to nought. His friends were away. Whatever *leetle thing* we had must be found elsewhere. So we went to a *trattoria*, where another of his friends, a serious, polite young man, who, we learned afterwards, owns the town and all the country thereabouts, sat and talked with us while we ate our lunch. Poor Sandrino! He had to pay for his English clothes and foreign friends! The *padrona*, backed by the *padrone* from the kitchen below, asked him no less than five francs for our macaroni and wine. A dispute, loud because of the distance between the disputants, followed ; but in the end Sandrino paid four francs, though half that sum would have been enough. It was some consolation for us to know that we, *forestieri*, had never been cheated so outrageously.

It was pleasant wandering through the town, with the grave young man as guide, to the Palazzo Communale, where the red and white flag of the Duke of Cornia waving outside was the same as that painted in the old frescoes within, and where councilmen, holding council, bowed to us as we passed ; and then to the old deserted castle which, with its grey battlemented walls and towers, was not unlike an English ruin. But it was pleasanter when, Sandrino having kissed his friend, we were on the road again, riding between yellow mulberries by the side of the lake. Sheep were grazing on the grassy banks. Donkeys and oxen were at rest in the meadows. But the peasants, mass heard, were at work again. Women on ladders were stripping the mulberries of their leaves; men on their knees were digging in the fields.

At the villa, Sandrino's friends were at home. At the gate the gay bicycler gave his war-cry. A young lady ran out between the roses and chrysanthemums in the garden and by the red wall where yellow pumpkins were sunning, to welcome him. Then her mother and sister came and also gave him greeting. They received us with courtesy. We were led into the drawing-room, a bare, barn-like place with cold brick floor, where there were three or four chairs, a table, an old piano, faded cretonne curtains hung on rough sticks at the windows, and small drawings pinned on the wall. A man in blue coat and trousers, such as the peasants wear, followed us in and sat down by the young ladies. He was one of her men, the *Signora* explained, and this was a house she had rented for the summer. Then we had the wine Sandrino promised, and we became very friendly. One of the daughters knew a little English, but when we spoke to her she hid her face in her hands and laughed and blushed. She never, never would dare to say a word before us, she declared. She was very arch and girlish. One minute she played a waltz on the piano; the next she teased Sandrino, and there was much pleasantry between them. The mother spoke French after a fashion, but when she had anything to say she relapsed into Italian. She lived in Rome, she said. We must come and see her there. But would we not now stay at her villa all night, instead of in Cortona? Then she squeezed my hand. "*Vous êtes bien sympathique!*" she said, and I think she meant to compliment me. Her husband, it seems, was a banker in Rome, and would be pleased, so she told us through Sandrino's interpretation, to do anything and everything for us.

Mother and daughters, men and maids, all walking amiably together, came to the garden-gate with us. The *Signora* here squeezed my hand a second time. The skittish young lady said "good-bye" and then hid behind a bush, and her sister gave us each some roses. It was here, too, we were to part with Sandrino. He must be in Montepulciano by six. More friends were coming. Would we write him postal cards to tell him of the distance and time we made? And that map of Tuscany we said we would give him, would we not remember it? He was going to take some great rides, and it would help him. Then we turned one way, and he, riding

On the Hill.

his best for the young ladies, the other, to be seen by us no more.

It was roses all the way to Cortona. They grew in villa gardens and along the road up the mountain; there were even a few among the olives, on the terraces whose stone supports make the city look from below as if it were surrounded by many walls instead of one only. Near the town we met two young lovers, their arms around each other's waists, and a group of men who directed us in our search for the inn up a short steep hill leading away from the main road. Above, inside the city gate, several other citizens told us we must go down again, for the road we had left led right by the door of the inn. Clearly the Albergo della Stella, for that was its name, was not well known in Cortona. After a climb of three miles it was provoking to go even a foot out of our way, and we turned back in no cheerful mood. It was disheartening, when, having come to the inn, we found the lower floor, by which we entered, the home of pigs and donkeys and oxen. The Major was right, I thought; Cortona was a rough place. The contrast when on the third floor of this establishment we were shown into a large clean really well-furnished room, with window overlooking the valley, made us neglect to drive a close bargain with the *padrona*, a neglect for which we suffered later.*

* Road from Montepulciano to Cortona good and generally level—long coast out of the former, three miles' climb into the latter.

LUCA SIGNORELLI'S TOWN.

The principal event of our stay in Cortona was a hunt for Luca Signorelli's house. Why we were so anxious to find it I did not know then, nor do I now; but we were very earnest about it. At the start a youth pursued us with the persistence of a government spy. It was useless to try and dodge him. No matter how long we were in churches or by what door we came out, he was always waiting in exactly the right place. In our indignation we would not ask him the way, but we did of some other boys, who forthwith led us such a wild-goose chase that I think before it was over there was not a street or corner of the town unvisited by us. We next employed an old man as guide. Of course he knew all about Luca Signorelli. He could show us all his frescoes and pictures in Cortona. Some of them were bad enough, as he supposed the *Signore* knew; they were painted in the artist's youth. But we wanted to see his house. Ah! we had but to follow him, and he led us in triumph to that of Pietro da Cortona. As this would not do, he consulted with an old woman who recommended a visit to a certain *padre*. The *padre* was in his kitchen. He had never heard of Signorelli's house, and honestly admitted his ignorance. But could he show us some fine frescoes or sell us antiquities? This failing, our guide hunted for some friends who, he declared, knew everything. But they were not in their shop, nor in the *caffè*, nor on the *piazza*, and in despair he took us to see another priest. The latter wore a jockey-cap and goggles, and was a learned man. He had heard of a life of Signorelli by a German. He had

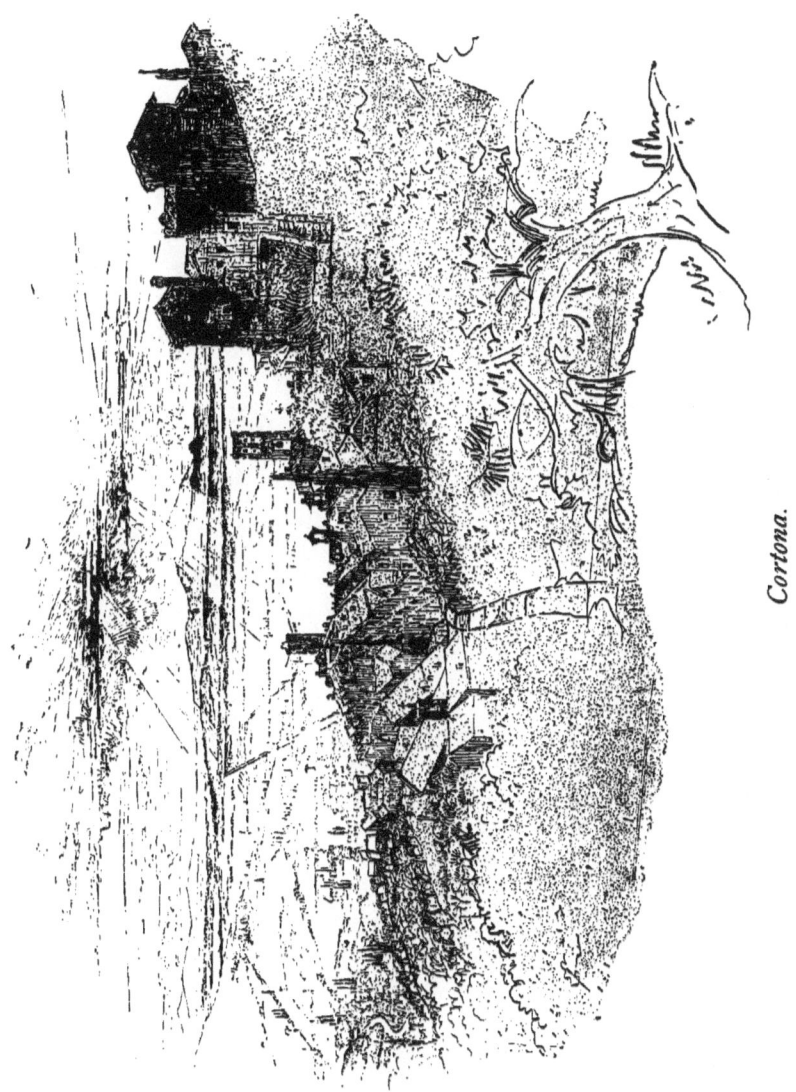

Cortona.

never read it, nor indeed could he say where it was to be had; but he knew there was such a book. He was certain our hunt was useless, since Signorelli had lived in so many houses the city could not afford to put tablets on them all, and so not one was marked. He himself was a professional letter-writer, and if the *Signore* had any letters he wished written—? We then gave up the search and dismissed the old man with a franc, though he declared himself still willing to continue it. It was in this way we saw Cortona.

For the last few days we had begun to be haunted by the fear of the autumn rains. If they were as bad as Virgil says, and were to fall in dense sheets, tearing the crops up by the roots while black whirlwinds set the stubble flying and vast torrents filled ditches and raised rivers, the roads must certainly be made unrideable. Since the morning we left Monte Oliveto the weather had been threatening, and now in Cortona there were heavy showers

As we sat in our room at the *albergo* after our long tramp, and J—— made a sketch from the window, we saw the sky gradually covered with dark clouds. The lake, so blue yesterday, was grey and dull. The valley and the mountains were in shadow, save where the sun, breaking through the clouds, shone on a small square of olives and spread a golden mist over Monte Amiata. Before J—— had finished the gold faded into white and then deepened into purple, and we determined to be off early in the morning.

TO PERUGIA:
BY TRAIN AND TRICYCLE.

THE next day I was tired and in no humour for riding. J—— wanted once to try the tricycle without luggage over the Italian roads. It was settled then between us that I should go alone by train to Perugia, where we should meet. Before seven we had our breakfast and the *padrona* brought us her bill. Because we had not bargained in the beginning she overcharged us for everything, but we refused to pay more than was her due. There was the inevitable war of words, more unpleasant than usual because the *padrona's* voice was loud and harsh and asthmatic. She grew tearful before it was over, but finally thanked us for what we gave her and asked us to come again so gently that we mistrusted her. I thought it as well to wait with the bags at the station, though my train did not start till eleven.

It was a beautiful coast down the mountain between the olives, four miles with feet up. The clouds had rolled away during the night, and it was bright and warm at the station when J—— left me to go on his way. It was quiet, too, and for some time I was alone with the porters. But presently a young woman with a child in her arms, came by. She stopped and looked at me sympathetically. I spoke to her, and then she came nearer and patted me on the shoulder and said, "*Poverina!*" It seems she had seen J—— bring me to the station and then turn back by himself. I do not know what she thought was the trouble, but she felt sorry for me. She was the wife of the telegraph operator and lived in rooms above the station. She took me to them, and then she brought me an illustrated Italian translation of *Gil Blas* to look at, while she made me a cup of coffee. Every few minutes she sighed and said again, "*Poverina!*" She gave me her card—Elena Olas, *nata* Bocci, was her name. I wrote mine on a slip of paper, and when the train, only an hour late, came, we parted with great friendship.

A regiment of soldiers was on its way to Perugia and made the journey very lively. Peasants, who had somehow heard of its coming, were in wait at every station with apples and chestnuts and wine, over which there was much noisy bargaining. At other times the soldiers sang. As the train carried us by the lake, from which the mountains in the distance rose white and shadowy and phantom-like; and by Passignano, built right in the water, with reeds instead of flowers around the houses, where fishermen were out in their boats near the weirs; and then by

Maggiore and Ellora on their hill-tops, I heard the constant refrain of the soldiers' song, and it reminded me of my friend at Cortona, for it was a plaintive regret for "*Poverina mia.*" Then there came a pause in the singing, and a voice called out, "*Ecco*, Perugia!" I looked from the carriage window, and there far above on the mountain I saw it, white and shining, like a beautiful city of the sun.

At the station J—— met me. He had been waiting an hour, having made the thirty-six miles between Cortona and Perugia in three hours and a half. He had had his adventures too. Beyond Passignano he met a man on foot who spoke to him and to whom he said "*Buon giorno!*" "Good morning," cried the man in pure insular English, and J—— in sheer astonishment stopped the tricycle. The tramp, for tramp he was, explained that he was an Englishman and in a bad way. He had been in Perugia with a circus which had had little or no success, and the rascally

Piping down the Valley.

Frenchman who managed it, had broken it up and made off, leaving him with nothing. He was now on his way to Florence where he wanted to be taken on by Prince Strozzi who kept English jockeys. But in the meantime he was hungry and had no money and must tramp it all the way. J—— gave him a franc for his immediate wants. He looked at the money. He supposed he could get a little something with it, he grumbled. He really was grateful, however, for he offered to push the machine up a hill down which he had just walked. But J——, telling him to hurry on, engaged instead the services of a small boy who was going his way. For pay he gave the child a coast down the other side into his native village, than which *soldi* could not have been sweeter. Did not all his playmates see him ride by in his pride?

Arriving in Perugia, J—— himself was a hero for a time. Many officers with their wives were in the station, and in their curiosity so far forgot their usual dignity as to surround him and beset him with questions as to his whence and whither, and what speed he could make. It is a long way from the station up the mountain to the town, but we went faster than we had ever climbed mountain before, for we tied the tricycle to the back of the diligence. J—— rode and steered it, but I sat inside, ending my day's journey as I had begun it, in commonplace fashion. The driver was full of admiration. We must go to Terni on our *velocipede,* he said, for in the mountains beyond Spoleto we would go down-hill for seven miles. *Ecco!* no need of a diligence then.

Very fair road from Cortona to Perugia; but the new one, Cortona—Castiglione del Lago Perugia—though longer, is more level and easier going.

AT PERUGIA.

THE *padrone* of the *albergo* at Perugia was a man of parts. He could speak English. When we complimented him on a black cat which was always in his office, he answered with eyes fixed on vacancy, and pausing between each word like a child saying its lesson: "Yes–it–is—a–good–cat. I–have–one–dog–and four–cats. This–cat–is–the–fa–ther–of–the–oth–er–cats. One–are–red–and–three–is–white." And when we had occasion to thank him, he knew enough to tell us we were very much obliged.

But we gave him small chance to display his powers. There was little to keep us in the inn when after a few minutes' walk we could be in the *piazza*, where the sun shone on Pisano's fountain, and on the palace of the Baglioni and the *Duomo* opposite. But what a fall was there! A couple of *gendarmes*, priests walking two by two, a few beggars, were the only people we saw in this broad *piazza*, where at one time men and women, driven to frenzy by the words of Fra Bernardino, spoken from the pulpit by the *Duomo* door, almost fell into the fire they had kindled to burn their false hair and ornaments, their dice and cards; and where at another, Baglioni fought, with the young Raphael looking on, to paint later one at least of the combatants; and where the beautiful Grifonetto lay in death agony, the avengers of his murdered kinsmen waiting to see him die, the heads of his fellow assassins looking grimly down from the palace walls, and Atalanta, his mother, giving her forgiveness for the deed for which but yesterday she had cursed him. In the aisles of the *Duomo* once so stained with the blood of

Baglioni that they had to be purified with wine before prayers could again be offered in them, a procession of white-robed priests and acolytes, bearing cross and censer, passed from one chapel to another before a congregation of two or three old women. It was the same in the narrow streets; all is now still and peaceful, where of old Baglioni, single-handed, kept back the forces of Oddi, their mortal foes. Only the memory of their fierceness and prowess remains; though I have two friends who say that in the dark street behind the palace, where brave Simonetto and Astorre fought the enemy until corpses lay in piles around them, they one night heard voices singing sadly as if in lamentation; and these voices led them onwards under one archway and then another until suddenly the sounds ceased. But when they turned to go homewards, lo! they had lost their way. The next morning they returned that they might by daylight see whence the music could have come. But all along the street was a blank wall. None but spirits could have sung there, and what spirits would dare to lift their voices in this famous street but those of Baglioni?

It must be the degeneracy of modern warriors that sets these heroes of the old school to singing lamentations. The Grifonettos and Astorres who feasted on blood, could they return to life and their native town, would have little sympathy with the captains and colonels who now drink tamarind water in the *caffè*, booted and spurred though the latter be. The *caffè* is everywhere the lounging-place of Italian officers, but in Perugia it seemed to be their headquarters. There was one on the Corso, a few doors from the palace, which they specially patronised. They were there in the morning even before the shops were opened, and again at noon, and yet again in the evening, while at other times they walked to and fro in front of it, as if on guard. But though the youngest as well as the oldest patronised it, the distinctions of rank between them were observed as scrupulously as Dickens says they are with the Chatham and Rochester aristocracy. The colonel associated with nothing lower than a major, the latter, in turn, drawing the line at the captain, and so it went down to the third lieutenant, who lorded it only over the common soldier. On the whole I think the lesser officers had the best of it; for whether they ate cakes and drank sweet drinks, or played cards, they were always sociable and merry. Whereas, sometimes the colonel sat solitary in his grandeur, silent except for the few words with the boy selling matches as he hunted through the stock to find a box with a pretty picture.

We were long enough in Perugia to carry the *Abate's* letters to San Pietro. The monks to whom they were written were away, but a third came in their place and gave us welcome. He showed J—— the inner cloister, to which I could not go. Women were not allowed there. It was because of my skirts, he said; and yet he, too, wore skirts, and he spread out his cassock on each side. While they were gone I waited in the church. I wonder if ghostly voices are ever heard within it. The monks, long dead, whose love and even life it was to make it beautiful until its walls and ceilings were rich and glowing, its choir a miracle of carving, and its sacristy hung with prayer-inspiring pictures, have, like the Baglioni, cause to bewail the degenerate latter day. The beauty they created now lives but for the benefit of a handful of monks, whose monastery is turned into a Boys' Agricultural School, and for the occasional tourist. Later from the high terrace of the park opposite San Pietro we saw the boys in their blue blouses digging and hoeing in the fields under the olives, where probably the monks themselves once worked. There is in this little park an amphitheatre with an archway, bearing the Perugian griffin in the centre. It is shaded by dense ilex-trees, from whose branches a raven must once have croaked; for evil has come upon the place, as it has upon the grey monastery so near it. Instead of nobles and knights and men-at-arms and councillors of state, two or three poor women with their babies sat on the stone benches gossiping. And as we lingered there in the late afternoon there came from San Pietro the sound not of monks chanting vespers, but of some one playing the "Blue Danube" on an old jingling piano. Only the valley below, and the Tiber winding through it, and the mountains beyond are unchanged!

ACROSS THE TIBER TO ASSISI.

WHEN we left Perugia in the early morning, we passed first by the statue of Julius II., thus receiving, we said to each other, the Bronze Pontiff's benediction. We imagined this to be an original idea; but it is useless to try to be original. Since then we have remembered the same thought came to Miriam and Donatello when they made the statue their trysting-place. Then we rode through the *piazza*, where a market was being held, and where at one end a long row of women, all holding baskets of eggs, stood erect, though all around other women and even men, selling fruit and vegetables, sat comfortably on low stools. Out on the other side of the Porta

Perugia---The Bronze Pontiff's Benediction.

Romana we saw that while Perugia was bright and clear in the sunlight, a thick white mist covered the valley, so that it looked as if a great lake, bounded by the mountains, lay below. The chrysanthemums and marigolds, hanging over high garden walls, and the grass by the roadside glistened with dew. Shining silver cobwebs hung on the hedges. Before many minutes, so fast did we go, we were riding right into the mist. We could see but a few feet in front of us, and the olives on either side, through the heavy white veil, looked like spectres. We passed no one but a man carrying a lantern and a cage of owls. It seemed but natural that so uncanny a ride should lead to a home of shadows. And when we came to the tomb of the Volumnii at the foot of the mountain, we left the tricycle without, and went down for a while into its darkness and damp. When we came out the mist had disappeared and the road lay through sunshine.

A little farther on we had our first near view of the Tiber. We crossed it by the old Ponte San Giovanni, so narrow that there was not room enough for us to pass a boy and donkey just in front. J—— called, and the boy pushed his donkey close to the stone wall; but for all that we could not pass. Even as he called he was stopped by a sudden pain in his side, the result probably of his descent into the tomb while he was still warm, for he had back-pedalled coming down the mountain. And so we waited many minutes on the bridge to see, not the yellow Tiber one always hears about, but a river blue in mid-stream, white where it came running over the mill-wheel and down the dam, and red and yellow and green where it reflected the poplars and oaks, and the skirts and handkerchiefs of the women washing on its banks. But after the bridge we left the river, for we were bound for Assisi. We had a quiet peaceful ride for several miles on the Umbrian plain, where in the old times no one dared to go without the permission of the Baglioni, between vineyards and fields where men were ploughing, and through insignificant little villages, and until we came out upon the large *piazza* in front of Santa Maria degli Angeli. It was crowded with peasants, for market was just over, and there came from every side the sound of many voices. When we rode by we were surrounded at once, two or three men keeping close to our side to sing the praises of the hotels at Assisi and shower their cards upon us. They pursued us even into the church and as far as the little hermitage beneath the dome, to tell us that each and all could speak English.

If the Umbrians about Assisi were always like this, Saint Francis was a wise man to hide himself in the woods and to make friends with beasts and birds. Over the sunny roads beyond Santa Maria, where he and Fra Egidio walked singing and exhorting men and women to repentance, we wheeled imploring, or rather commanding, them to get out of the way. It was a hard pull up the mountain-side, the harder because the great monastery on its high foundations seemed always so far above us. When almost at the city gate a monk in brown robes, the knotted cord about his waist, passed. He stopped to look, but it was with a frown of disapproval; I think Saint Francis would have smiled.

Perfect road.

Assisi—A frown of disapproval.

AT ASSISI.

IT was just noon when we reached Assisi, but we rode no more that day. We spent the afternoon in the town of Saint Francis. The *albergo* we selected from the many recommended was without the large cloisters of the monastery. The *cameriere* at once remembered that J—— had been there before, though eighteen months had passed since his first visit. The *Signore* had two other ladies with him then, he said. He was delighted with the *velocipede*. It was the first time in all his life he had seen one with three wheels. Nothing would do but he must show us the finest road to Rome. He spread our map on the table, as we eat our dinner, and put on his glasses for he was a little bad in the eyes, he explained, and then he pointed out the very route we had already decided upon. *Ecco!* here between Spoleto and Terni, we should have a long climb up the mountain, but then there would be seven miles down the other side. Ah! that would be fine! This long coast to Terni was clearly to make up for the hardships we had already endured on toilsome up-grades.

After dinner we went to the church. Goethe, when he was in Assisi, saw the old Roman Temple of Minerva, and then, that his pleasure in it might not be disturbed, refused to look at anything else in the town and went quickly on his way. But when I passed out of the sunlight into the dark lower church and under the low, rounded arches to the altar with Giotto's angels and saints above, it seemed to me he was the loser by his great love for classic beauty. Many who have been to this wonderful church have written descriptions of it, but none have really told, and indeed no one can ever tell, how wonderful it is. The upper church, with its great lofty nave and many windows through which the light streams in on the bright frescoed walls, is beautiful. But this lower one, with its dark subdued colour and its dim light and the odour of incense which always lingers in it, is like the embodiment of the mystery and love that inspired the saint in whose honour it was built. In it one understands, for the first time perhaps, what it is for which the followers of St. Francis give up life and action. Whoever were to be long under the influence of this place must, I thought, always stay, like an old grey-haired monk, kneeling before a side altar, rapt in contemplation. And yet on the very threshold I found three or four brothers laughing and joking with two women—Italian Dr. Mary Walkers they must have been, for they wore men's collars and cravats and coats with field glasses slung over their shoulders, and stiff felt hats, and they were smoking long *cigari Cavour*. They were artists and had been painting, Oh so badly! in the church all the morning.

The sun was setting when we left the monastery and walked through the streets, now silent and deserted, where Francis in his gay youth wandered with boon companions, singing not hymns, but love songs. A small boy came and walked with us, and unbidden acted as our guide. Here was the *Duomo*, he said, and here the Church of Santa Chiara; and, when we were on the road without the city gate, *Ecco!* below Santa Maria degli Angeli. For, from where we stood, we looked down upon the huge church rising from the plain, where even now there are scarcely more houses than in the days when Franciscans, coming from far and near to hold counsel with their founder, built their straw huts upon it. Our self-appointed guide was a bright little fellow and never once begged like other children who followed us.

So when he showed us the road to Foligno, where we must ride on the morrow, J—— gave him a sou. At the door of the *albergo* he said he must go home, but not to supper; he never had any. He asked at what time we should leave in the morning, when he would like to come and say good-bye. "*Felice notte*"—a happy night—were his last words as he turned away.

VIRGIL'S COUNTRY.

THE next morning, with a select company of ragged boys, our young guide arrived in time to see us start. When I came out he nodded in a friendly way, as if to an old acquaintance, to the wonder and admiration of the other youngsters. The waiter, his glasses on, came to the gate with us. Two monks, standing there, asked how far we were going on our *velocipede*. "To Rome?" they cried; "why then we are two priests and two pilgrims!" Our guide and his friend ran down the mountain-side after us until we gave the former another sou, when they at once disappeared. It seemed a little ungrateful, but I did not give him much thought, for just then J—— bade me back-pedal with all my might. The machine went very fast despite my hard work, and to my surprise J—— suddenly steered into a stone pile by the road-side. "The brake is broken," was his explanation as we slowly upset.

Fortunately, however, the upright connecting the band of the brake with the handle had only slipped out of place, and though we could not fix it in again securely, J—— could still manage to use it. This, as far as we could see, was the one defect in our tricycle, but defect it was. A nut on the end of the upright would have prevented such an accident. But this is one of the minor particulars in which tricycle-makers—and we have tried many—are careless. We had the rest of the coast without interruption. Half way down our little friend and his followers ran out from under the olives; he had taken a short cut that he might see us again.

From Assisi to Terni was a long day's ride

by towns and villages, through fair valleys and over rough mountains. From the foot of the mountain at Assisi, past Monte Subasio, which, bare and rocky, towered above the lower olive-covered hills, the road was level until we rode by Spello with its old Roman gateway and ruined amphitheatre. But the hill here was not steep, and then again there came a level stretch into Foligno, the first lowland town to which we had come since we left Poggibonsi, and which, with its mass of roofs and lofty dome rising high above the city walls, looked little like the Foligno in Raphael's picture. Already in our short ride, for it is but ten miles from Assisi to Foligno, we noticed a great difference in the people. It was not only that many of the women wore bodices and long ear-rings, and turned their handkerchiefs up on the top of their heads, but they, and the men as well, were less polite and more stupid than the Tuscans or the Umbrians about Perugia. Few spoke to us, and one woman to whom we said good morning was so startled that she thanked us in return, as if unused to such civilities. For all J——'s shouts of *a destra!*—to the right —and *eccomi!* they would not make room for us; and now in Foligno one woman, in her stupidity or obstinacy, walked directly in front of the machine, and when the little wheel caught her dress, through no fault of ours, cried "*Accidente voi!*" the *voi* being a far greater insult than the wishing us an accident. Then she walked on, cursing in loud voice, down the street, by the little stream that runs through the centre of the town and into the market-place, where St. Francis in mistaken obedience to words heard in ecstasy, sold the cloth he had taken from his father that he might have money to re-build the church of San Damiano. Even the beasts we met were as stupid as the people. At our coming horses, donkeys, and oxen tried to run. We therefore looked for at least a light skirmish when, beyond Foligno, a regiment of cavalry in marching order advanced upon us. But the soldiers stood our charge bravely. Only the officer was routed and retreated into the gutter. Then, forgetting military discipline, he turned his back upon his men to see us ride.

We were now on the old Via Flaminia and in the valley of Clitumnus, Virgil's country. The poet's smiling fields and tall, stiff oaks, his white oxen, and peasants behind the plough or enjoying the cool shade, were on either side. Crossing the fields were many stony beds of streams, now dry, lined with oaks and chestnuts, under whose shade women were filling large baskets with acorns and leaves. The upturned earth was rich and brown. Through the trees or over them we saw the whitish-blue sky, the purple mountains, some pointed like pyramids, and the gray olive hills with little villages in their hollows, and before long Trevi on its high hill-top. And

Gathering Leaves.

then we came to the Temple of the River God, Clitumnus, of which Pliny writes, and where the little river, in which Virgil says the white flocks for the sacrifice bathed, runs below, an old mill on its bank and one willow bending over it.

At the village of Le Vene, near the source of the stream, we stopped at a wine-shop to eat some bread and cheese. There was no one there but the *padrone* and a dwarf who wore a decent suit of black clothes and a medallion of the Pope on his watch-chain. He had come in a carriage which waited for him at the door. I think he was a drummer. He drank much wine, and spoke to us in a vile *patois*. Indeed, the people thereabouts all spoke in dialects worse, I am sure, than any Dante heard at the mouth of Hell. He had travelled and had been in Florence, where he had seen a *velocipede*, but not like ours. It was finer, or perhaps, he should say, more commodious. The seats were side by side, and it had an umbrella attached, and it was worked by the hands. It went, oh, so fast! and he intimated that we could not hope to rival its speed. I suppose our machine without an umbrella seemed to him like a ship without a sail. But I think he had another tale to tell when, ten minutes later, he having started before we did, we passed him on the road. We were going so fast, I only had time to see that in his wonder the reins fell from his hands.

Then came the small, wretched village of San Giacomo, with its old castle built up with the houses of the poor, and then Spoleto, where we lunched in a *trattoria* of the people, which was much troubled by a plague of flies. A company of *bersaglieri*, red caps on the back of their heads and blue tassels dangling down their backs, sat at one table, ordering with much merriment their soup and meat and macaroni to be cooked *a la bersagliere*. At another two young men were evidently enjoying an unwonted feast. And at the table with us were three peasants, one of whom had brought his bread in his pocket. He ate his soup for dessert, and throughout the meal used his own knife in preference to the knife and fork laid at his place. Two dogs, a cat, and a hen wandered in from the *piazza*, and dined on the bits of macaroni dropped by the not over-careful soldiers. The *cameriere* greeted us cordially. He too had a machine, he said, but had never heard of a *velocipede* with three wheels. His had but two; the *Signore* must see it. And before he would listen to our order for lunch, he showed J—— his bicycle, a bone-shaker. He was very proud of it. He had ridden as far as Terni. Ah! what a beautiful time we should have before the afternoon was over. Seven miles down the mountain!

The thought of this coast made us leave Spoleto with light hearts, though we knew that first must come a hard climb. But if the road was as perfect as it had been all the morning, there was not much to dread. It was half-past two when we started from the *trattoria*, but we were fifteen minutes in walking to the other end of the town. There was no use riding. The streets were narrow and steep and crowded with stupid men and women and donkeys and officers, who instead of controlling were controlled by their horses. Beyond the gate the ascent at first was gradual and we rode easily, even as we worked looking back to the famous old aqueduct and the shadowy heights of Norcia. For some distance we went by the dried-up bed of a wide stream, meeting many priests on foot and peasants on donkeys. But as the way became steeper we left the stream far below, and came into a desolate country where the mountains were covered with scrub oaks, and priests and peasants disappeared. Only one old man kept before us, making short cuts up the mountain side, but after a while he too rode out of sight. We soon gave up riding. J—— tied a rope to the tricycle and pulled while I pushed. The sun was now hidden behind the mountain and the way was shady. But still it was warm work and wearisome; for before long the road became almost perpendicular and was full of loose stones. How much more of this was there? we asked a woman watching swine on the hill-side. "A mile," was her answer, and yet she must have known there were at least three. Finally, after what seemed hours of toiling, we asked another peasant standing in front of a lonely farm-house how much farther it still was to the top. "You are here now," she said. She at least was truthful. A few feet more and we looked down a road as precipitous as that up which we had come, and so winding that we could see short stretches of it, like so many terraces, all the way down the mountain. We walked for about a hundred yards, and it was as hard to hold back the machine as before it had been to push it. Then we began to ride, but the strain on the brake loosened the handle a second time. We dismounted, and J—— tried to push it back into place. It snapped in two pieces in his hands. Here we were, eight miles from Terni in a lonely mountain road in the evening—the sun had already set—with a brakeless machine which, if allowed to start down hill with its heavy load of two riders and much luggage, would soon be more unmanageable than a runaway horse. The seven miles coast to which we had looked forward for days was to be a walk after all. Like the King of France and his twenty thousand men, we had marched up the mountain that we might march down again. Is it any wonder that we both lost our tempers, and that an accident was the smallest evil we wished the manufacturers of our tricycle? Because they cared more for lightness than for strength, since record-making is as yet the chief end of cycling, the necks of people who ride for pleasure are forsooth to be risked with impunity!

However there was nothing to do but to walk into Terni. It was very cold, and we had to put on our heavy coats. Presently the moon rose above the mountains on our left. By its light we could see the white road, now provokingly good, but steep and winding and all unknown, the hills that shut us in on every side, and, far below, the stream making its way through the narrow pass. The way was unpleasantly lonely and silent; now for an hour or more we went wearily on without hearing a sound but our steady tramp; and now we passed a farm-house within which many voices were raised in anger, while from the barn a dog barked savagely upon our coming. At times we thought we saw in the distance a castle with tall towers or an old ruin, but when we drew near we found in its place great rocks and cliffs of tufa. Once we went through a small village. The way here was not so steep, and for a few minutes we rode. Just beyond the houses three men, driving home a large white bull, walked in the middle of the road. J—— shouted that they might give us more space to pass. But they only laughed and tried to set the bull on us with loud cries of *Via!* Before the last died away we were walking again.

On and on we walked, all the time holding back the tricycle. But at last we began to meet more people. Men with carts and donkeys went by at long intervals, but they spake never a word, and we too were silent. Now and then we heard the near tinkling of cow-bells, and came to olive gardens, where in the moonlight the black, twisted trunks took grotesque goblin shapes, and the branches threw a network of shadows across our path. Then we came to a railroad, and we knew we were at the foot of the mountains, and that Terni was not far off. We were at the end of the seven miles' coast and could ride again.

Two men just then coming our way, J—— asked them how far we were from the town. But they stood still and stared for answer. A second time he asked, and still they were speechless, and we left them there, dumb and motionless. Not far beyond the road divided, and on either side were a few houses. A woman, or a fiend in female form, sat in front of one. "Which is the way to Terni?" we asked. She was silent. Once more we asked. "*Chi lo sa?*"—who knows?—she answered. This was more than tired human nature could endure. J—— turned upon her with an arrangement in popular Italian, that conquered her as the prayers of St. Anthony vanquished her sister demons. She arose and meekly showed us the way.

In another minute the lights of Terni were in sight. Then we wheeled by a foundry with great furnace in full blast, up a broad avenue with rows of gas-jets, to the gates of the city, to find them shut. There was a second of despair, but J—— was now not to be trifled with, and he gave a yell of command which was an effectual "Open, Sesame." And so we rode on through lively streets and *piazza* to the hotel, to supper and to bed.

TERNI AND ITS FALLS.

WE know little of Terni, except that the hotel is so cold that the *cameriere* comes into the dining-room in the morning with hat on and wrapped in overcoat and muffler, and that there is an excellent blacksmith in the town, for the next morning, as soon as J—— had had the brake mended, he paid the bill and brought out the tricycle. The *padrone* was surprised at the shortness of our stay. Did we not know there were waterfalls, and famous ones too, but three miles distant? We could not take the time to visit them? Well, then, at least we must look at their picture, and he showed us a chromo pasted on the hotel omnibus. I am afraid he took us for sad Philistines.

But the fear of another kind of waterfall was still a goad to hurry us onwards. Now we were so near our journey's end, no wonder, however great, could have led us from the straight path.

IN THE LAND OF BRIGANDS.

THERE was a great *festa* that day, and all along the street and out on the country road we met men and women in holiday dress, carrying baskets and bunches and wreaths of pink chrysanthemums. In Narni, on the heights which Martial called inaccessible, men were lounging in the *piazza* or playing cards in the *caffè*. For the shepherds alone there was no rest from every-day work. Before we reached even Narni, but ten miles across the valley from Terni, we saw several driving their sheep and goats into the broad meadows. They wore goat-skin breeches, and by that sign alone we should have known we were nearing Rome. We lunched at Narni on coffee and cakes, for it was the last town through which we should pass on that day's ride. It was here Quintus, in its Roman prosperity, stayed so long that Martial reproached him for his wearisome delay. Could he come to it now, I doubt if his friend would have the same reason for complaint. It did not seem an attractive place, and when we asked a man about the country beyond, he said it was "*bruto.*" We did not learn till afterwards that this applied to the people, and not to the country, and that here we ought to have been briganded.

We were now high up on the mountain, on one side steep rocks, on the other a deep precipice. Far below in a narrow valley ran the little river Nar, and on the bank above it the railroad. It was not an easy road to travel, and often the hills were too steep to coast or to climb. The few farm-houses by the way were closed, for the peasants had gone to church. We saw an occasional little grey town crowning the top of sheer grey cliffs, like those in Albert Dürer's pictures, or an old castle either deserted or else with farm-house built in its ruins, where peasants leaned over the battlemented walls. But the only villages through which we rode were Otricoli, just before we descended to the valley of the Tiber, where we created so great a sensation that an old woman selling chestnuts, cooked, I think, by a previous generation, was at first too frightened to wait on us; and Borghetto, on the other side of the valley, where we saw in the *piazza* the stage from Civita Castellana, in which town we were to spend the night.

There were a few people abroad. In the loneliest part of the mountain an old man in a donkey-cart kept in front of us on a long up-grade. Interested in the tricycle, he forgot the donkey, which gave up a straight for a spiral course, and monopolised the road. J—— angrily asked its driver which side he meant to take. But the old man heaped coals of fire on his head by offering to carry us up in his waggon. After we left him far behind we passed two travellers resting by the wayside. Their bags lay on the ground, and they looked weary and worn. They gave us good day, and where were we going, they of course wanted to know. They too were bound for Rome, it turned out, and had come from Bologna. After the two gentlemen of Bologna we overtook a group of merry peasants, coats slung over their shoulders for no possible reason but for the sake of picturesqueness, and hats adorned with gay pompons of coloured paper and tinsel. One carried branches of green leaves and red fruit like cherries, and as we went by he gave us a branch and wished us a good journey. Next went by an old woman who said with a smile that we could go without horse or donkey—a witticism heard so often it could no longer make us laugh. And then a little boy, all alone, came piping down the valleys wild.

We went with much content over the plain by the Tiber, where there were broad grassy stretches full of sheep and horses, and here and there the shepherds' gipsy-looking huts. It was such easy work now that we ate our chestnuts as we rode; but beyond the bridge, on which Sixtus V. and Clement VIII. and Gregory XIII. have, in true papal fashion, left their names, the hills began again. On we toiled, beneath shady oaks and by rocky places, until we came out on a wide upland. From the treeless road the meadows rolled far beyond to high mountains on whose sloping side the blue smoke of charcoal-burners curled upward. The moon had already risen, and in the west the setting sun filled the sky with glowing amber light, against which the tired peasants going home were sharply silhouetted.

We were glad to see Civita Castellana. One or two men in answer to our questions had told us we were close to it, but we did not believe them. The fields seemed to stretch for miles before us, and there was not a house or tower in sight. But suddenly the road turned and went down-hill, and there below was the city perched on tufa cliffs, a deep ravine surrounding it. Two *carabinieri*, in cocked hats and folded cloaks like the famous two solitary horsemen, were setting out on their night patrol. Vespers were just over in the church near the bridge, and along the way where happy little Etruscan school-boys once whipped homewards their treacherous schoolmaster, little Italian boys and girls let loose from church ran after us, torturing us with their shrill cries. Soon their elders joined them, and we were closely beset with admirers. The town, too, was in a hubbub about us, and in the streets through which we wheeled men and women came from their houses to follow in our train. At the door of the *albergo*, where we were detained for several minutes, the entire population collected. We had difficulty in getting a room. The *festa*, the *padrone* said, had brought many country people into the town, and the inns were full to overflowing If J—— would go with him he would see what could be done for us. The search led them through three houses. In the meantime I kept guard over the machine. It was well I did, for when J—— had gone the natives closed upon me. Toddling infants and grey-haired men, ragged peasants and gorgeous officers pushed and struggled together in their desire to see. Every now and then a stealthy hand was thrust through the crowd and felt the tyre or tried the brake. I turned from left to right, crying *Guarda! Guarda!* I lifted exploring hands from the wheels. But in vain. What was one against so many? A man sitting in the doorway took pity on my sad plight. He came out and with a stick mowed the people back. Then J—— returned, having found a room in the first house, which the *padrone* had thought fit to conceal until the last.

A MIDDLING INN.

THE *albergo* of Civita Castellana was but a "middling inn." The *padrone*, in English tweed, high boots and Derby hat, looked half cockney, half brigand. His wife wore an elaborate false front and much lace about her neck. But they were far finer than their house. We were lodged in the garret, in a room the size of a large closet. The way to it led through another bed-chamber, long and low, in which four cots were ranged in a row along the wall. When we crossed it on the way down stairs to dinner, I devoutly prayed that on our return four night-caps would not be nodding on the pillows. Later in the evening when we had dined we strolled out to the *piazza*. To see the life of an Italian town you have only to go to the *caffè*. We went to one near the *albergo*. There were two tables in it. We sat at the smaller, and at the other were four ragged boys playing cards.

Fortunately we were the first to go to bed in the garret. All through the night, however, for the mattress was hard and I slept little, I heard loud snores and groans, and the sound of much tossing to and fro. We rose early in the morning, but when we opened our door the cots were empty, .though they had not been so long.

ACROSS THE ROMAN CAMPAGNA.

EARLY as we were, the whole town was stirring when we came down stairs. But who ever knew the hour when the people of an Italian town were not up and abroad? No sooner did J—— bring the tricycle from the stable, where it had been kept all night, to the *albergo*, than the *piazza* was again crowded. On they all came with us, men, women, and children, hooting and shouting, jumping and dancing through the vilely paved streets and finally sprawling over the walls and on to the rocks beyond the gate.

There they all stayed until we had gone down the hill, over the bridge crossing the stream at its foot, and up the hill on its opposite side, passing from their sight round the first curve. Soon we were on an upland, and now really at the beginning of the Campagna. The morning was cold. For many miles we rode through a champaign gleaming white with frost. But as the sun rose higher in the heavens, and the yellow light, which had at first spread over the sky, faded and left a clear blue expanse above, the air grew warmer and the frost disappeared. The road wound on and on between oak woods and wide, cultivated fields, and green grassy plains which gradually changed into great sweeps of rolling, treeless country, like the moors. By the roadside were thick bushes of low green sage and tangled blackberries, and in places the broad flagstones of the old Flaminian Way, with weeds and dandelions and pretty purple flowers growing from the crevices. Sometimes a paving of smaller stones stretched all across the road, so that for a minute or two we were badly shaken, or else, coming on them suddenly

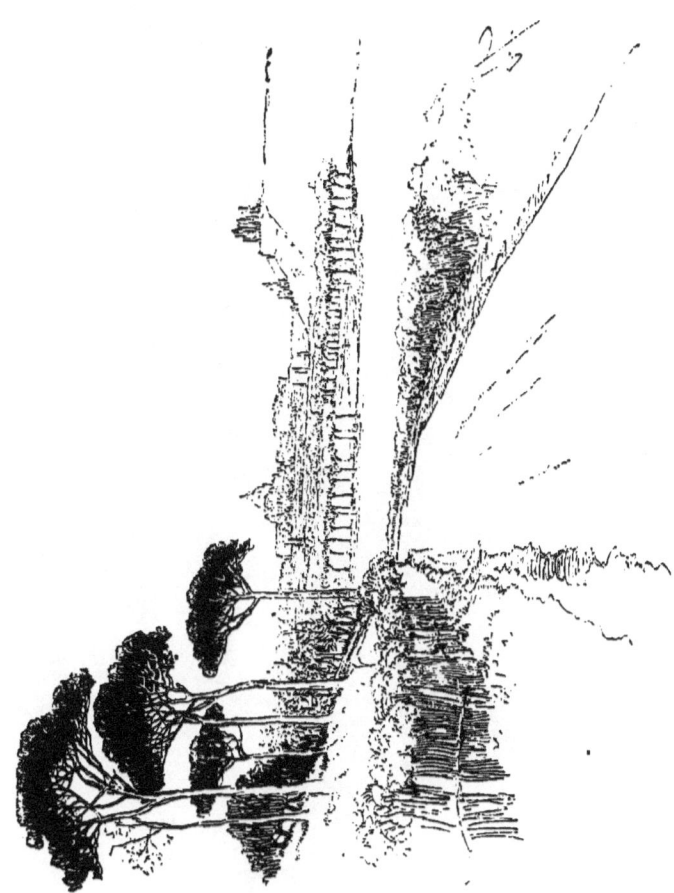

From Via Flaminia, near Ponte Molle.

at the foot of a hill, all but upset. Truly, as has been said, it could have been no joke for the old Romans to ride. To our left rose the great height of Soracte, not snow-covered as Horace saw it, but bare and brown save where purple shadows lay. At first we met numbers of peasants, all astride of donkeys, going towards Civita Castellana, families riding together and eating as they went. Later, however, no one passed but an occasional lonely rider, who in his long cloak and high-pointed hat looked a genuine Fra Diavolo; or else sportsmen and their dogs. It is strange that though we saw many of the latter, we never once heard the singing or chirping of birds. There were hill-sides and fields full of large black cattle, or herds of horses, or flocks of sheep and goats. There were shepherds, too, sleeping in the shade, or by the roadside leaning on their staffs or ruling their flocks with rod and rustic word as in the days when Poliziano sang. And if there was no bird's song to break the silence of the Campagna, there was instead a loud baaing of sheep, led by the shrill, piercing notes of the lambs. If it was to such an accompaniment that Corydon and Thyrsis sang in rivalry, their songs could have been poetical only in Virgil's verse.

How hard we worked now that our pilgrimage was almost ended! We scarcely looked at the little village through which we wheeled, and where a White Brother was going from door to door, nor at the ruins which rose here and there in the hollows and on the slopes of the hills; and when at last we saw on the horizon the dome coming up out of the broad, undulating plain, we gave it but a short greeting and then hurried on faster than ever. We would not even go to Castel Nuovo, which lies a quarter of a mile or so from the road, but ate our hasty lunch in a *trattoria* by the wayside, while a man, an engineer he said he was, showed us drawings he had made on his travels, and asked about our ride. How brave it was of the *Signora* to work, he exclaimed, and how brave of the *Signore* to sketch from his *velocipede!* And after this "the hills their heights began to lower," and with feet up we went like the wind, and every time we looked at the dome it seemed larger and more clearly defined against the sky. But about six miles from Rome our feet were on the pedals again and we were working with all our might. Sand and loose stones covered the road, which grew worse until, in front of the staring pink quarantine building, the stones were so many that in steering out of the way of one we ran over another, and the jar it gave us loosened the screw of the luggage-carrier. We were so near Rome we let it go. This was a mistake. But a little farther, and the whole thing gave way and bags and knapsack rolled in the dust. It took some fifteen minutes to set it to rights again; and all the time we stood in the shadeless road, under a burning sun, for the heat in the lower plains of the Campagna was as great as if it were still summer. As the luggage-carrier was slightly broken, we were afraid to put too great a strain upon it, and for the rest of the journey the knapsack went like a small boy swinging on behind.

Like those other pilgrims, we were much discouraged because of the way. But at last, wheeling by pink and white *trattorie*, whose walls were covered with illustrated bills of fare, and coming to an open place where street-cars were going and coming, the Ponte Molle, over a now yellow Tiber, lay before us, and we were under the shadow of the dome we had from afar watched for many hours. Over the bridge we went with cars and carts, between houses and gardens and wine-shops, where there was a discord of many hurdy-gurdies, to the Porta del Popolo, and so into Rome. *Carabinieri* were lounging about the gate, and carriages were driving

Stop!

to the Pincian; but we rode on and up the street on the right of the *piazza*. When we had gone a short distance we asked a man at a corner our way to the Piazza di Spagna. We should have taken the street to our left, he said, but now we could reach it by crossing the Corso diagonally. As we did so we heard a loud *sst, sst* behind us, and we saw a *gendarme* running up the street; but we went on. When we wheeled into the Piazza di Spagna, however, a second, almost breathless, ran out in front of us, and cried, "Stop!" But still we rode. "Stop!" he cried again, and half drew his sword. In a minute we were surrounded. Models came flying from the Spanish steps; an old countryman carrying a fish affectionately under his arm, bootblacks, clerks from the near shops, young Roman swells—all these and many more gathered about us.

"Stop!" the *gendarme* still cried.

"Why?" we asked.

And then his fellow-officer, whom we had seen on the Corso came up. "Get down!" he said in fierce tones of command.

"Why?" we asked again.

"*Per Christo!*" was his only answer.

The crowd laughed with glee. Hackmen shouted their applause. It was ignominious, perhaps, but the wisest policy to get down and walk to our hotel.

THE FINISH.

WHAT pilgrim of old times thought his pilgrimage really over until he had given, either out of his plenty or his nothing, in alms? Two months later we too gave our mite, not to the Church or to the poor, but to the Government; for we were then summoned before a police magistrate and fined ten francs for "*furious* riding on the Corso, and refusing to descend when ordered!"

And so our pilgrimage ended.

THE STONES OF ROME.

THE STONES OF ROME.

"Roma, Roma, Roma,
Non è piu come era prima!"

It may seem to many readers that we made our Italian Pilgrimage for the sake of the ride. It is true we rode because we knew there could be no more beautiful journeying to Rome, and to show that, though every one now does go by rail, this one beautiful way at least is left. It is as true that we now hope we are the forerunners of a long succession of tricycling pilgrims to wheel over the old Flaminian Way, through the Porta del Popolo, into the streets of the Eternal City. Moreover it may be we take pride in the fact that we were the first of these pilgrims, foolishly wondering if our record must altogether die like other records of a day. We have at all events the consolation of knowing that it was made for our pleasure and not as an advertisement. But when all is said the truth still remains that our tricycle was but the means to a greater end. Though we enjoyed ourselves on the road, seizing each day as it came, from the moment we left Florence—or, for that matter, from the moment we left London—we were looking forward, with as much reverence as did pilgrims of other days and faiths, to the first glimpse of the great dome shaping itself above the swells of the Campagna, to lifting the heavy leather curtain and breathing the incense-laden air of the house of St. Peter, to wandering into the Ghetto and so into mediæval Rome, and, perhaps more than all, to stepping back into the world of the Cæsars and emperors on the Capitol or the Palatine, in the Forum or the Coliseum. And so, our pilgrimage over, our tricycle sold and our fine paid, we settled down for four months in the city we had come to see, and endeavoured to make the best of its brand-new prosperity before which the things of the past are so fast disappearing.

It was in the old church of the Aracœli, which stands where was once the Arx of the Romans, and which is built with columns and marbles brought from Pagan temples and palaces, that Gibbon, as he listened to the vesper chants of the monks, the modern successors of ancient warriors, first thought of writing his history. To those who have, with him, eyes to see, there is not a street, not a corner of the seven-hilled city, which will not appeal as strongly, which will not speak, as it did to him, of the death of the old, the growth of the new. In the stones of Rome the story of the decline and fall of the great empire is written more clearly than in the most eloquent pages of the historian. It is told even where the life of modern Romans is brightest and busiest, and where but few traces remain of the past. It is the lesson you learn when you linger on the Pincian while the band plays, and watch the people—the monks and soldiers, the tourists and models, the nurses and children, the students from the Propaganda and the long lines of schoolboys—and then remember that it was here Lucullus had his villa in which he supped in state with Lucullus; and that here, later, were the gardens of Messalina, where now she danced as a Bacchante, with her lover as Silenus and her attendants as Satyrs, and where again, the storm from Ostia having broken overhead, she crouched in her despair to await the death-blow which, despite her mother's exhortations, she was too cowardly to give herself. It is the chapter you read when you walk along the Corso, and compare the careless crowd aimlessly wandering up and down, or lounging about the *caffè*, with the throng that came forth to meet the conquerors from the north as they marched over the same road, then the Flaminian Way, and under the triumphal arches there raised in honour of their victories. It is the beginning and end of the reflections awakened within you as you pass from streets full of bustle and activity to the silence and desolation of the Forum and the Palatine.

But on the Corso and the Pincian it is through the imagination that these contrasts are realised. In the Forum and on the Palatine the bare brick walls, the broken columns, and the defaced arches, are expressive witnesses of the mighty fall that is there. But they are now guarded with care and respect, as the last years of a once powerful monarch, who has grown too old to reign, and who has suffered the many slings and arrows of outrageous fortune, might be protected by new rulers of a younger generation, and the reverence thus shown them continually recalls their former greatness. It is when buildings and monuments, when temples and theatres and tombs, raised by emperors and patricians, have either been allowed to sink into neglect and contempt worse than actual ruin, or else, instead of being reverentially set apart, have been adapted to their modern surroundings, that the changes wrought by time are most marked. Not, however, in the sense that they are noticed at once. In many cases the old has been made so completely subservient to the new that it is only by degrees its age and original purpose are remembered. When, for example, you first look at the little baker-shop at the corner of the Via della Croce Bianca and the Via Alessandrina, and where of old was the Forum of Nerva, you wonder at the caprice which made such a building into such a shop, before you become conscious that those columns, half buried by the street, and by happy chance spared when Paul V.—as true a barbarian as any Genseric or modern syndic—destroyed and carried off five others to decorate his fountain on the Janiculum, once formed part of the portico of a temple of Minerva; that those sadly worn bas-reliefs on what was the entablature probably represent the priests who,

A Baker's Shop.

in women's robes and with womanly occupations, waited on, and honoured the goddess in her temple at Albano. Or, when you walk out to the church of St. John Lateran, your attention is called to the stages and street-cars coming and going in the *piazza* and the street beyond, to the peasants and soldiers and perhaps monks gathered near the wine-shops opposite, before you remember that the high brick arches, between which the wine-shops are built, belong to the old Aqua Claudia, through which Claudius sent water flowing from far Subiaco, for miles over the Campagna, into Rome ; that the Obelisk, by which street-cars and stages pass all day long, records the power of Constantius, who brought it to grace the pleasure-grounds of Romans, from where in Thebes it stood before the Temple of the Sun. But the changes here are in the end more striking from the fact that the past is thus absorbed in the every-day life of the present, and is at first so easily ignored. Would not the fall of a monarch from his high estate—to continue the simile already used—seem much sadder if, instead of being cared for in his old age, he was forgotten and lost sight of in the midst of a vile rabble with whom he had been forced to make his home?

It is for this reason there is no place in all Rome full of such strange significance as the Ghetto.* At its very entrance its story is told by

---

* It may be well to add a note here to explain that these impressions were written in 1885. Only a year ago! and yet in that time Rome has seen so many changes that it is no longer the Rome we knew. We hear that the old picturesque, tumble-down wilderness of the Ghetto has blossomed out as a fresh modern rose; that the dirty high houses rising from the river have given way to a fine new embankment; that the ruins of the Theatre of Marcellus and Portico of Octavia have been, or are to be, carefully restored to the condition in which they were left, not by their builders, but by Savelli and Orsini, and the warring Vandals of mediæval Rome. I suppose this is all as it should be, but to those who knew and loved the old wilderness, the new promenade will be one of the saddest of sad wastes and desolate places. It is not merely the Ghetto that has suffered from the enthusiasm of municipal barbarians. The Ponte Rotto has gone. What is Scipio Africanus, or Æmilius Lepidus to modern Romans? Old ilex groves and cypress hedges have been replaced by neat rows of stupid houses. Victor Emmanuel, instead of grey monastery walls, looks down

In the Ghetto.

a tall, narrow, grey house, which rises above the lower houses on either side, as if to concentrate the attention of the passer-by on itself. It is very shabby and forlorn, and at all hours ragged, bare-footed children play at its foot, and frowsy-headed women lean out of the windows and scream, in Roman fashion, to their neighbours. It seems even shabbier and more forlorn because of the signs it gives of better days; for on its lower story, directly on the ground, is an old Roman archway, now all built up; above is a Gothic window, particularly noticeable in Rome, where almost all Gothic forms have been so carefully destroyed, while just beneath the roof are ordinary modern square windows, whose battered, disreputable green shutters bang to and fro with every

from the Capitol over the Corso——But why go on? The trouble is we wretched *forestieri*, who do not have to spend our lives in cities of the past, have no sympathy with United Italy's strivings after modern comfort, cleanliness, and common-place mediocrity. Where the people during a public demonstration—paid, it is whispered, for loyalty—cry "Long live King Humbert!" we outsiders, with interests elsewhere, cry instead, "Would that Victor Emmanuel and Humbert had never lived!"

breeze. The vicissitudes of fortune through which the Ghetto has passed are much the same as these which are here typified. In it the extremes of ancient wealth and power, and of modern misery born of mediæval and priestly oppression, meet. It is the lowest quarter in the city, the one in which the poverty, and dirt, and squalor, so long shut in by barred gates and high walls, still linger, though walls and gates have been removed. There, in streets so narrow and lined with houses so high that they are chill and damp even when the sun shines at midday, and which are often overflowed for days at a time by the Tiber, live the Jews, now as in the time of their slavery, the most wretched of the Roman population. Side by side with their dreary, shabby houses, or but a few steps from them, are the ruins of buildings erected in the palmiest days of the empire. It is as if Whitechapel had taken possession of Westminster; the Bowery of Fifth Avenue. And it is because

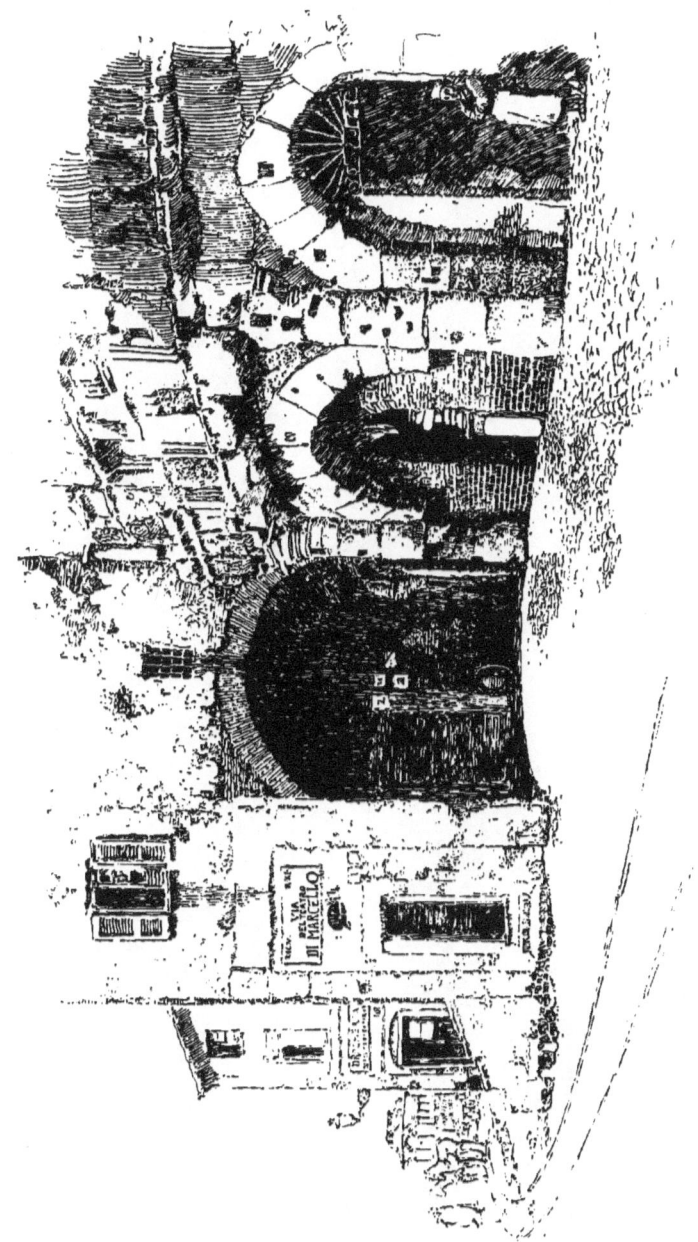

The Theatre of Marcellus.

their greatness is unfelt by the many people living in or near them that these ruins are more truly desolate than the empty Coliseum or Baths of Caracalla, though in the latter in summer-time wild flowers grow and birds sing undisturbed.

Just on the outskirts of the Ghetto, and close to the Piazza Montanara, where the blue-cloaked, brigand-hatted peasants congregate, is one of the most melancholy of these wrecks of former grandeur. It was once the Theatre of Marcellus, built by the mourning Augustus, on foundations laid by Julius Cæsar, to the memory of his young nephew, the husband of his daughter, and his chosen successor, who died, however, before he could attain the power his uncle destined for him. When the Farnese prince, Paul III., made a quarry of the theatre, part of the outer wall was fortunately untouched, and this is now standing. But it is blackened and begrimed, and bears testimony to the varied fortunes through which the building has passed since that first day, nineteen hundred years ago, when thousands gathered within to see the games and wild-beast fights, and gladiatorial combats, held for its dedication. Other, even fiercer, contests which followed in after years, left their marks upon it. For when Romans, their thirst for warfare not yet quenched, ceased to fight the enemy abroad, to fight each other at home; and when Frangipani were safely ensconced in the neighbouring Coliseum, and behind the Arch of Titus, Orsini in the Theatre of Pompey, and Crescentii in the tomb of Hadrian, Pierleoni, and then Savelli, sought their stronghold in the Theatre of Marcellus, its walls, had they been less strong, could not have withstood more successfully the assaults, then directed against them, than they did later the attacks of Paul III.'s army of destroyers. As it is, in those portions which still remain, the heavy blocks of stone, every here and there, have disappeared to be replaced by bricks, making a strange patchwork, while the columns, in places, have sunk deep into the walls, and their capitals have gone entirely.

Where the amphitheatre had been, the same Savelli, the rivals of the Orsini and the bitter enemies of the papal power until it was given to one of their own family, finally built their palace. There was no nobler house in Rome than these fierce Ghibellines. They ranked with Colonna, Conti, and Orsini. Every year it was their right to set free a criminal sentenced to death, no matter what his crime or by whom condemned. But the last of their line died in the seventeenth century, and, by a curious freak of fortune, their palace became the property of the Orsini, their once deadly foe, who thus peaceably obtained the building which, when it had been a fortress, they had many times vainly tried to gain by force. Niebuhr lived here when he was in Rome, in what had been the third story of the ancient theatre, and in rooms from which he could look below on to the orange-trees, and jessamines, and vines, which had sprung up on the soil watered by blood of mediæval knights, of lions and tigers, and of gladiators.

The entrance to the palace is towards the river, and, though the porter who stands in the gateway wears in his cocked hat the colours of another family, the Savelli bears still keep guard above him on the tall gateposts, the old name still survives in the near Via di Monte Savelli. But it is on the other side that the ancient walls are now to be seen. Here is no well-kept carriage-road lined with soft grass-plots, watched by a porter, and over which only carriages of aristocratic guests pass. Following the curve of the building is a narrow, somewhat dirty street, full of people, peasants from the Piazza Montanara, and Jews from the Ghetto, and within its lower arches, between the Doric pillars, are small shops. These are dark enough, for the only daylight which reaches them is from the street without, and it fades away into gloom a few feet beyond the threshold. Therefore the tradesmen, who are of the lower rank, to suit their customers, set out their wares in the open air, that all who go by may see them. The dealer in second-hand furniture spreads far beyond his archway his beds and chairs and tables, in every pitiful stage of dilapidation, and hangs above them his rusty dented pots and pans. Next to him a butcher has his stall, and from the blocks of travertine dangle joints and pieces of meat of shape elsewhere unknown. A few steps farther on is a *trattoria*, in which from morning till night men sit at the little tables eating and drinking, but most often only talking. Then comes a blacksmith's shop. The fire in its farthest corner is the brightest spot in the gloomy row, the hammering of the workmen the loudest noise in the noisy neighbourhood; so that in the memories you carry away with you from a visit to the

Theatre of Marcellus, a blacksmith, instead of mighty emperor or youthful hero, stands out the central figure.

And as you turn to the *piazza* beyond, on the road over which once rolled Titus and Vespasian, in their chariots in triumphal procession, with their rich spoils of gold, and silver, and precious stones, of seven-branched candlesticks, and tables of the law from the Temple of Jerusalem, most eloquent of all their proofs of victory, borne before them, you see a horse-car track, and the car which has just arrived from, or is just starting to, San Paolo beyond the walls. Instead of sound of trumpets, and clang of armour, you hear the conductor's horn loudly blowing.

Horse-cars in Rome are as incongruous as steamboats in Venice, and under the very shadow of a building founded by Julius Cæsar are even more out of place than in the modern broad, characterless Via Nazionale. Their usefulness, however, more than compensates for

Temple of Vesta.

their incongruity, and, indeed, a ride in them is interesting as well as useful, if only for the contrasts between old and new Rome which it constantly suggests; for soon after they leave the theatre, they run by the old round Temple of Vesta—a temple to which its modern name of Santa Maria del Sole is as inappropriate as its Corinthian columns to the mean, wooden roof which they now support.

After the Temple of Vesta, the track lies for some distance at the foot of the Aventine, and then, with a sudden turn, passes through an archway, where, a surprise perhaps to those who have not come guide-book in hand, is the pyramid of Caius Cestius. By it, but at a little distance from the road, is the Protestant Cemetery, where Keats and Shelley are buried. It is a quiet place, notwithstanding the close proximity of barracks and stoneyard, and full of the sad peacefulness which the presence of the dead seems always to bring with it. A fosse runs round the little graveyard, as if to separate it the better from the outer world, and within stand tall cypresses, like sentinels. In the spring and summer violets and roses cover the mounds and gravestones, and even as early as January pale pink daisies dot the grass. Beyond is the Porta San Paolo, of old the Porta Ostiensis, with its mediæval, battlemented towers, and to the right is the grey pyramid, which still serves as tomb to the tribune in whose honour it was raised, while mausoleums of emperors have been put to uses vile. Thus it has come to pass that, just as the brick battlements of mediæval Rome, and heavy stonework laid in far earlier ages, exist together in the same gateway, so the dead of the ancient world and of the modern — he who ordered his body after death to be wrapped in precious stuffs, and he whose tomb, at his own desire, declares that his name was writ in water —lie side by side.

Scarcely less significant, in its own way, is Monte Testaccio, which you see at some

Here lies One whose Name is writ in Water.

little distance before you as you turn from the quiet graves towards the city again. It is an artificial hill, formed of broken pottery. But it is well worth while climbing to the top; for after you have passed by the shining pink and white houses at its foot, entrances to the wine-cellars, which run like catacombs beneath it, and have scrambled by a little narrow path rough with broken bits of pots and jars, to the cross on its summit, you look forth across the broad plain of the Campagna. It stretches on one side, with the yellow Tiber winding through it, to the white sea-line on the horizon, and in front to the soft purple hills, on whose slopes Marino, Albano, and Tivoli gleam like patches of sunlight. Your eyes cannot but follow the sweep of the hills as they rise and fall, as if to show the shadowy, white-topped Appenines beyond until they reach the many peaks of tall Soracte. They will not rest there long, however, for on this side, just below, is Rome herself, with her domes and here and there a lofty bell-tower springing up high above her brown, red, and yellow roofed houses. As you look, it will seem to you as if in the days when proud emperors played with the elements, and made lakes, and planted forests in the centre of the city, they must also have raised this hill, that ever after men, who saw from it the surpassing loveliness of the land over which they ruled, might feel their power. But Monte Testaccio is really the growth of chance, though no one now knows exactly why or when the old pottery was thrown there. It may be that merchants, unloading vessels just arrived from Africa or farther Spain, pitched into this one great heap the jars which, because of rough waves and storms, had come to them in pieces. It may be that the *plebs* on the near Aventine made this their refuse-heap. One thing alone is certain, that while rare marbles and precious metals were being scattered far and wide, so that Rome again became a city of brick, as Augustus had found it, the odds and ends of pottery which no man, not even the most destitute, cared for, were preserved until they had accumulated into a goodly pile, as if Fate had built a lasting monument to her own inconstancy.

But there are other ruins just without the Ghetto which are no less striking than those of the Theatre of Marcellus. If, instead of taking the horse-car, you leave the theatre by the Via del Teatro di Marcello, you will see at its farther end, an old brick arch, through which and the two arches beyond you look into another narrow crooked street, winding between high houses from whose windows clothes for ever hang. Above these arches are, here, great blocks of stone, which would fall apart were it not for strong iron clamps which hold them together; and here, blackened brick walls, in every nook and cranny of which weeds are growing, and which are overlooked by the upper stories of the houses built close to them. On the near flat, irregular roofs, more clothes, some bright yellow and red, are always drying in the sunlight. Within the enclosure made by the archways and a small church, which forms the fourth side of the square, are columns forlornly mutilated, some standing apart, others imbedded in the wall. Without, in the old *Pescheria*, or fish-market, are heavy marble slabs, and about the shabby doors of still shabbier houses are strips of marble, with here and there a cracked and stained relief.

These are all that remain of the beauty and grandeur of perhaps the noblest of all the many noble buildings once standing hereabouts, and which made Strabo say of this quarter of the city, then the Circus Flaminius, that the rest of Rome seemed but a mere supplement to it. It was because it already gave signs of this splendour in the latter days of the Republic that Cæcilius Metellus came to it after his victories in Macedonia, to erect a portico which, like his new name Macedonicus, would commemorate his triumphs, and which would at the same time be a fit setting for the bronze

Porta Octavia, with Roman Fish Stalls.

statues of Lysippus he had brought back with him as spoils. It was in restoring its first splendour, much impaired by fire and neglect during years of civil war, that Augustus built upon the site of the Portico of Metellus the Portico of Octavia, in honour of his sister. This building was destined to be the scene in one age of an emperor's triumph, and in another of a priesthood's cruelty; to be appropriated now to the pride of tyrants, degenerate descendants of ancient patricians, and now to the wrath of patriots incensed against them. For it was here that Vespasian and Titus came to celebrate their conquest of Israel, Josephus mingling with the crowd of courtiers, and noting all the pomp and ceremonial, of which he was afterwards to write the account for future ages. And it was here, too, to the Church of San Angelo, which had taken the place of marble temples of Jupiter and Juno, that later generations of the Jews, then vanquished, were pricked through the streets like hounds, that the Christians, whom they had helped to their sins, might, as Browning says, help them to their God!

On the walls and arches of the same Portico the semi-barbarians of mediæval Rome painted their *stemme*, as proud of their so-called noble blood as heroes among their ancestors were of great deeds of patriotism. And close to these armorial bearings Rienzi painted the famous allegory of his triumph over the haughty Roman barons. "I see the time of great justice; do thou await that time!" was inscribed beneath. One wonders if he would think that time had come now that frescoes, his, as well as theirs, have faded away, leaving only traces of their once bright colours, now that the building that nobles were proud to claim as theirs is shamefully dishonoured by its surroundings. What Colonna or Orsini to-day would care to raise his standard on this crumbling pile? The old ragged skirt waving from a tiny window in the bricks over a defaced

Corinthian capital is the true banner of the neighbourhood. Cobblers sit at work by the side of imperial marbles, above which dangle long strings of onions, and a feeble light burns before a picture of the Madonna. From the church in which Rienzi assembled the people who had not yet lost their dream of freedom, now come the poorest of Rome's many poor, whose only conscious need is that of *soldi*, whose only struggle is one with their own poverty. On the spot where was found the Medicean Venus, the Roman's ideal of female loveliness, now crouch old hags, digging in the refuse of the Ghetto, and looking up with a smile and a triumphant " *Trovato!* " as they pick out scraps of food which men but a degree less miserable have thrown away. These are the successors of Cæsars and mediæval princes in the Portico of Octavia. It is easily understood why Ampère called it one of the most remarkable ruins of Rome, one showing the strongest contrast between past and present in this city of contrasts.

This French scholar was always deeply impressed by the places in which ancient and modern Rome are brought so closely together that, paradoxical as it may sound, the wide gulf which separates them is only made to seem the wider. He was struck as forcibly by the Ponte Rotto as by the Portico of Octavia, from which it is not far distant. "Scipio Africanus and a suspension-bridge! here is one of those contrasts only to be found in Rome!" he exclaims, in speaking of this bridge, of old the Pons Æmilius, begun by Æmilius Lepidus and finished by Scipio Africanus, swept away by the Tiber and rebuilt by Popes, until the latter, tired of a contest in which they were always worsted, left it for many years broken, thus giving it its modern name, and then finally connected the uninjured arches by the present chain bridge. And if you look from the Ponte Rotto down the river when the tide is low, you can see, not far off, fragments of massive masonry, said to be, though Ampère doubts the fact, ruins of the Pons Sublicius, built by

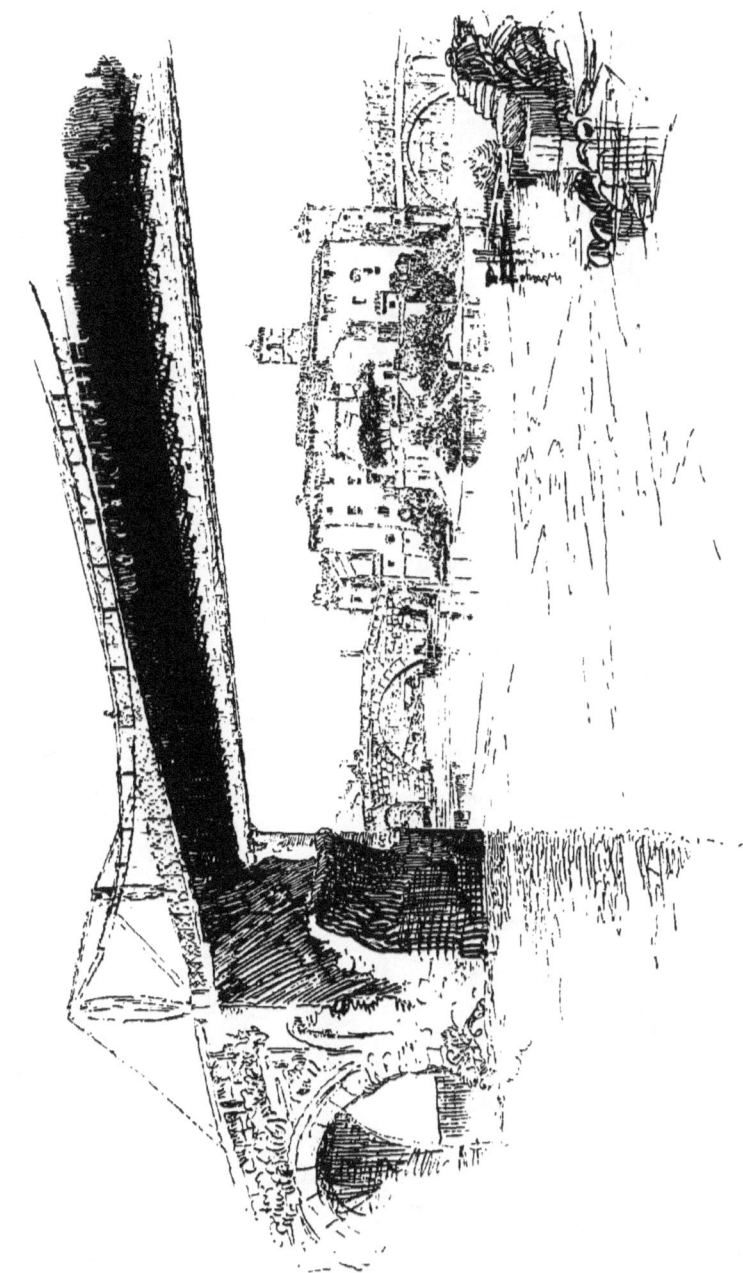

The Ponte Rotto.

the grandson of Numa Pompilius, kept by Horatius in the brave days of old, and already ancient when Æmilius Lepidus undertook his work! Who, however, but an occasional tourist or scholar, in looking at these fragments, thinks of the past or cares for the dim ages when there were still Sabine kings in Rome, and Romans prayed to their father Tiber! The men and women who see them almost daily are as indifferent to them as the bright lemon-trees growing on a terrace near the Tarpeian Rock are to the centuries' old archway and heavy wall just below them.

But merely to point out all these contrasts would be to write the history of the City of Rome. They confront you at every step. There is scarcely a city gateway through which you pass in or out where the memories of other days do not thicken upon you, so that the presence of the modern customs official seems an impertinence; at the Porta del Popolo, and the Porta San Sebastiano, because through them you go beyond to the great northern and southern military roads; at the Porta Maggiore, because remains of old aqueducts there commemorate the victories of Dentatus over Pyrrhus, while inscriptions record the work of great emperors—and so on with the others. If you come to the city in the railway train, itself an anomaly in the capital of the Cæsars, it will carry you into a station by the side of which still stands, though broken and towerless, part of the wall of Servius Tullius, much of which, indeed, was pulled down, as if it had been useless rubbish when the station was built. While it is yet in sight you drive or walk by the brick wreck of the Baths of Diocletian, to find it encircling the tents and waggons, the merry-go-rounds and shooting galleries, of travelling showmen. Posters of petty Italian Barnums decorate walls whose splendour once outshone even that of the Baths of Caracalla and of Titus. It is the same wherever you go. The tomb of a

Wash Day at Tivoli.

Hadrian has become a common fortress, and the site of a famous Christian miracle; that of an Augustus, a circus ring, or the ball-room for children's carnival gaieties. Pieces of the ivy-grown aqueduct of a Claudius now serve as chief ornament in the garden of a modern villa; the Arch of Gallienus is used as a lounging place by peasants who, on St. Anthony's Day bring their donkeys to be blessed at the adjoining church of San Vito. In one monastery are the ruins of a Temple of Venus and Cupid; beneath another, the underground passages where wild beasts were kept for the Coliseum. Christian saints are honoured in the very buildings where Pagan heroes and heroines were worshipped; the feasts of the Virgin are celebrated on the very spot where of old were held the rites of Ceres and Proserpine. Water, brought from far mountains to fill imperial baths, flows into fountains where women come to wash their clothes; obelisks from the conquered East rise in squares which every year are given over to carnival follies or the din of the Befana Night. Nor do these contrasts cease in the Rome beyond the walls—in the Campagna and the near hill-towns. There, railway tracks run between the arches of aqueducts and telegraph wires over them; wine-shops and farm-houses are built in ancient tombs, and in Tivoli a Temple of Vesta is inclosed in the garden of an innkeeper, an advertisement to bring him custom.

Thus has it fared with the glory that was Rome. Her stones lie deep in the dust of ages. It seems as if, like Jerusalem in the Lamentations, the ancient city waits by the roadside of time to ask all those who go by to attend and see whether there has ever been sorrow like unto hers!

VETTURINO *v.* TRICYCLE.

VETTURINO *v.* TRICYCLE.

WHO has not journeyed through a country with his favourite author long before he makes the actual trip himself? and who, when he comes to see with his own eyes that at which he has hitherto looked through some one else's, does not find himself his best guide? Long before I came to Italy I had travelled along its highways and byways with many authors, more especially with Hawthorne in his *Italian Note-Book*, and Mr. Howells, in his *Italian Journeys* and *Venetian Life*. When it was finally my good fortune to make the journey, I was at first lucky enough to have for a companion not his books, but Mr. Howells himself; and I frankly confess I found him far more delightful and satisfactory in person than in print. A year later I started for the same country, this time encumbered with a wife and a tricycle. Mr. Howells could no longer be my *cicerone;* in the first place he was back in Boston—I might add, as if in parenthesis, calling me "lucky dog" for being able to go so soon again over the well-known ground; and, in the second place, because the route I now intended to take is not described in his books. But it is in Hawthorne's *Note-Book,* a volume which, as I have just said, I had frequently studied. But, of course, I forgot to put it in my knapsack, and so had not a chance to see it until I arrived in Rome. When I there looked into it, naturally in a more critical spirit—inspired by personal knowledge of the subject—than I ever had before, the first thing that struck me was the advantage I had had over my old master in travelling by tricycle instead of by carriage. From the little village of Passignano to Rome we had followed exactly the same road, and, though we began our rides at its opposite ends, I could

VETTURINO v. TRICYCLE.

still easily compare the time we had made, and the comfort and convenience and pleasure we had enjoyed by the way. As this comparison may be interesting to many who intend some day to make the cycling tour of Italy, I will here briefly indicate Hawthorne's experience, principally as to time and roads, and then mine :—

HAWTHORNE'S JOURNEY TO FLORENCE.	MY NOTES.
FIRST DAY OF TRIP.	LAST DAY OF TRIP.
We passed through the Porta del Popolo at about eight o'clock, and ... began our journey along the Flaminian Way. ... The road was not particularly picturesque. The country undulated, but *scarcely rose into hills*. ... Finally came to the village of Castel Nuovo di Porta ... between twelve and one. ... Afternoon, Soracte rose before us. ... The road kept trending towards the mountain, following the line of the old	We left Civita Castellana at a quarter to eight. Road so rough, had to walk downhill and up again. (So did Hawthorne's party.) Road very picturesque, and before long, a distant glimpse of St. Peter's. Began to see, and occasionally to feel, the paving of the old Flaminian Way, which is abominable. Made of flagstones worn into great ruts, or else little blocks, like the Roman pavement. Coming on a stretch of it, at the foot of a

Flaminian Way, which we could see at frequent intervals close beside the modern track. It is paved with large flagstones, laid so accurately together that it is still, in some places, as smooth and even as the floor of a church, and everywhere the tufts of grass found it difficult to root themselves into the interstices. . . . Its course is straighter than that of the road of to-day. . . . . I forget where we finally lost it. . . . Passed through the town of Rignano—road still grew more and more picturesque. . . . Came in sight of the high, flat table-land, on which stands Civita Castellana. . . . After passing over the bridge, I alighted with J. and R. and made the ascent on foot. . . . At the top our *vetturino* took us into the carriage again, and quickly brought us to what appears to be a very good hotel. . . . After a splendid dinner we walked out into the little town, etc., etc.

hill, and hidden with dust, smashed our luggage-carrier, and loosened the machine—more than the whole trip had done. Passed Rignano, —usual sensation—good *caffè*. Under Soracte all morning. Reached Castel Nuova di Porta at eleven. (Distance to this village from Civita Castellana much farther than from it to Rome, yet we reached it one hour sooner than Hawthorne did, starting out from Rome.) Road got worse and worse. Finally nothing but ruts and stones. Hills not to be laughed at (though Hawthorne thought them scarcely perceptible). Arrived at the Porta del Popolo about half-past one. (About three and a half hours' better time than Hawthorne.) Distance, thirty-five Italian miles.

SECOND DAY.

Roused at four o'clock this morning . . . ready to start between five and six. . . . Remember nothing particularly till we came to Borghetto. . . . After leaving Borghetto, we crossed the broad valley of the Tiber. . . . Otricoli by and by appeared. . . . As the road kept ascending, and as the hills grew to be mountainous, we had taken on two additional horses, making six in all, with a man and boy . . . to keep them in motion. . . Murray's guide-book is exceedingly vague and unsatisfactory along this route. . . . Farther on (we saw) the grey tower of Narni. . . . A long, winding street passes through Narni, broadening at one point into a market-place; . . . came out from it on the other side. . . . The road went winding down into the peaceful vale. . . . From Narni to Terni I remember nothing that need be recorded. Terni, like so many other towns in the

OUR SECOND DAY FROM ROME.

(We never got up at any such unearthly hours as Hawthorne indulged in.) Left Terni at eleven o'clock, having been obliged to get a new brake made. Terni, dead level, in low valley—straight, wide road, ten miles across the valley—surface of the road good. Just outside of Narni, road climbs up a steep hill into the town. (There must have been an earthquake since Hawthorne's time, as Terni, which he saw in a high and commanding position, now stands in the lowest part of the valley, with mountains all around.) From Narni up nearly all the way to Otricoli, with the exception of here and there such a steep descent that we had to hold the machine back with all our might; riding for several hours was almost impossible. (Wish we had had six horses, a man, and a boy to pull us on.) From Otricoli, down and all across the valley neighbourhood, stands in a high and commanding position. . . . We reached it between eleven and twelve... It is worth while to record, as history of *vetturino* commissary customs, that for breakfast we had coffee, eggs, and bread and butter; for lunch, an omelette, stewed veal, figs and grapes, and two decanters of wine; for dinner, an excellent vermicelli soup, two young fowls fricasseed, and a hind-quarter of roast lamb, with fritters, oranges, and figs, and two more decanters of wine.

excellent riding to Borghetto: then big hill, up out on to the Campagna, and up and down—good road—all the way to Civita Castellana, which we reached between six and seven. Terrible sensation! (This day Hawthorne came in two hours ahead; but he had six horses and the hills in his favour.) We eat every day coffee, bread and butter, or rolls in the morning; for lunch, a beefsteak, or macaroni, and fruit, *no wine*, but fresh lemons and water; for dinner, soup, two meats, fruit and a *fiasco* of wine—distance about thirty-three Italian miles. (We carried Baedeker, and not Murray, and found it not unsatisfactory.)

THIRD DAY.

At six o'clock this morning . . . we drove out of the city gate of Terni. . . . Our way was now through the vale of Terni. . . . Soon began to wind among steep and lofty hills. . . . Wretched villages. . . . At Strettura,

THIRD DAY.

Left Assisi about eight. Splendid coast down into the valley. Beautiful ride over the undulating road, past Spello to Foligno, not stopping in the latter place, excepting to have accidents wished us by an old woman we added two oxen to our horses, and began to ascend the Monte Somma, which.. is nearly four thousand feet high where we crossed it. When we came to the steepest part of the ascent, Gaetano *allowed us to walk.* . . . We arrived at Spoleto before noon. . . . After lunch . . . we found our way up a steep and narrow street that led us to the city gate. . . . Resumed our journey, emerging from the city into the classic valley of the Clitumnus. . . . After passing Le Vene, we came to the little temple . . . immortalised by Pliny. . . . I remember nothing else of the valley of Clitumnus, except that the beggars . . . were well-nigh profane in the urgency of their petitions. The city of Trevi seems completely to cover a high peaked hill. . . . We reached Foligno in good season *yesterday afternoon.* (This passage really belongs to his fourth day of travel, but as it shows at what time of the third day he reached Foligno,

we almost ran over. Then through the beautiful valley of the Clitumnus — grand road—lovely day and wonderfully fair country. (We saw no beggars.) Rode by the little temple spoken of by Pliny. Ate some bread and cheese at Le Vene. Reached Spoleto at one— lunched—then rode up the steep street, through the gate at the other end of the city, and then began a tremendous climb of six miles over Monte Somma, most of which we had to walk. At last had hard work to push. Coming finally to the top, found the descent on the other side even steeper. Where it was a little less steep, we got on the machine, put on the brake, which came off in my hand. Bad brake was the one defect in our tandem. Had to walk the rest of the way. In Strettura, men set bull on us. (Not quite so pleasant as Hawthorne's experience.) Arrived in Trevi at eight o'clock, having walked the last few miles by moon-

I have included it with the third.)

FOURTH DAY.

I have already remarked that it is still possible to live well in Italy at no great expense, and that the high prices charged to *forestieri* are artificial, and ought to be abated. . . . We left Foligno betimes in the morning . . . soon passed the old town of Spello. . . . By and by we reached Assisi. . . . We ate our *déjeûner*, and resumed our journey. . . . We soon reached the Church of St. Mary of the Angels. . . By and by came to the foot of the high hill on which stands Perugia, and which is so long and steep that Gaetano took a yoke of oxen to aid his horses in the ascent. We all, except my wife, walked a part of the way up. . . . The coach lagged far behind us.

light—about forty miles altogether, of which we walked fully the last fourteen. (Made in one day what Hawthorne did in a day and a half.)

FOURTH DAY.

(Expenses of this trip about five francs a day each.) Rode from Perugia to Assisi, a distance of fourteen miles, in about two hours. Splendid coast down the hill outside of Perugia (up which Hawthorne walked). Crossed the Tiber. Visited Santa Maria degli Angeli. Awful stitch in my side. Climbed up into Assisi, where we stayed all afternoon, to recover, and to see the church.

FIFTH DAY.

Left Perugia about three o'clock to-day, and went down a pretty steep descent. . The road began to ascend before reaching the village of Maggiore . . . between five and six we came in sight of the Lake of Thrasymene . . . then reached the town of Passignano. (He stayed there all night.)

SIXTH DAY.

We started at six o'clock . . (for Arezzo). We saw Cortona, like so many other cities in this region, on its hill, and arrived about noon at Arezzo.

FIFTH DAY.

I covered their fifth and sixth days' ride, this time by myself on the tricycle, in three hours and a half actual riding time, and was pulled up the long hill into Perugia, in a most easy and delightful way, behind the diligence.

From Arezzo, Hawthorne went directly to Florence in one day, over a road which Italian cyclers have told me is excellent, and which is the post-road to Rome. We went by way of Montepulciano and Siena, being between two and three weeks on the way. I hope this short account of about one-third of our ride may convince some people that cycling is far quicker than the old posting system, far pleasanter than riding in a stuffy railway carriage, which whirls you through tunnels, and far the best way in which to see Italy,— a country which abounds in magnificent roads, and which should be thoroughly explored by all cyclers who care for something beside record breaking.

THE END.

A LIST OF BOOKS PUBLISHED BY
SEELEY & CO.
46, 47 & 48, ESSEX STREET, STRAND, W.C.
(*LATE OF 54 FLEET STREET*).

PUBLISHERS OF THE PORTFOLIO, *an Artistic Periodical*.
Published Monthly. Price 2s. 6d.

THE PORTFOLIO; an Artistical Periodical. Edited by P. G. HAMERTON. Volume for 1886, 1*l.* 15*s.* or 2*l.* 2*s.*

Specimen of the Minor Illustrations in 'Imagination in Landscape Painting.'

IMAGINATION IN LANDSCAPE PAINTING. By P. G. HAMERTON. With Fourteen Copper Plates and many Vignettes. Price 21*s.*, cloth, gilt edges.

Large-paper Copies (75 only), price 4*l.* 4*s.* half morocco.

FINE ART BOOKS.

THE SAÔNE: a Summer Voyage. By P. G. HAMERTON. With many Illustrations by T. Pennell. 4to. price 12s. 6d. cloth.

Large-paper Copies (250 only), price 1l. 11s. 6d.

Specimen of the Illustrations in 'The Saône.'

PICTURESQUE ARCHITECTURE. Twenty Plates by Ernest George, Lalanne, Lhermitte, &c. &c. Imp. 4to. price 21s. cloth.

CAMBRIDGE. By J. W. CLARK, M.A. With Twelve Etchings and numerous Vignettes by A. Brunet-Debaines and H. Toussaint. Price 1l. 1s.

'A thoroughly artistic work of topographical description and illustration.'—*Illustrated London News.*

ETCHINGS IN BELGIUM. Thirty Plates. By
ERNEST GEORGE. New Edition. On hand-made paper,
imperial 4to. 1*l*. 1*s*.

'A book to be loved and prized by all to whom art is dear.'—*Standard*.

PRISON ROOM above the NORMAN TOWER.

WINDSOR. By the Rev. W. J. LOFTIE. With
Twelve Plates and very numerous Vignettes. Cloth, gilt edges,
price 21*s*.

Large-paper Copies, price 4*l*. 4*s*. half morocco.

FINE ART BOOKS. 5

THE ITCHEN VALLEY FROM TICHBORNE TO SOUTHAMPTON.
Twenty-two Etchings by HEYWOOD SUMNER. Price 1*l.* 11*s.* 6*d.*

'We heartily commend it to artists.'—*Athenæum.*

THE AVON FROM NASEBY TO TEWKESBURY.
Twenty-one Etchings by HEYWOOD SUMNER. Price 1*l.* 11*s.* 6*d.* Large-paper Copies, with Proofs of the Plates, 5*l.* 5*s.*

'Deserves high praise.'—*Academy.*

Specimen of the Minor Illustrations in 'Paris.'

PARIS IN OLD AND PRESENT TIMES,
with Especial Reference to Changes in its Architecture and Topography. By P. G. HAMERTON. With Twelve Plates and many Vignettes. Price 21*s.* cloth, gilt edges.
Large-paper Copies, price 4*l.* 4*s.* vellum.

AN ENGLISH VERSION OF THE ECLOGUES
OF VIRGIL. By the late SAMUEL PALMER. With Illustrations by the Author. Fourteen Copper-plates. Price 21*s.* cloth.

LANCASHIRE. By LEO H. GRINDON. With Fourteen Etchings and numerous Vignettes. Price 1*l*. 1*s*. Large-paper Copies, with Proofs of the Plates, 3*l*. 3*s*.

'Cannot fail to delight those who admire good artistic work.'—*Liverpool Daily Post.*

Specimen of the Minor Illustrations in 'Stratford-on-Avon.'

STRATFORD-ON-AVON, from the Earliest Times to the Death of Shakespeare. By SIDNEY L. LEE. With Fourteen Plates and Thirty-one Vignettes, by E. HULL. Price 21*s*. cloth, gilt edges. Large-paper Copies, price 4*l*. 4*s*., vellum.

'A really valuable and acceptable Christmas gift-book.'—*Guardian.*

FINE ART BOOKS.

MICHEL ANGELO, LIONARDO DA VINCI, AND RAPHAEL. By CHARLES CLEMENT. With Eight Illustrations on Copper. Price 10s. 6d.

ISIS AND THAMESIS: Hours on the River from Oxford to Henley. By Professor A. J. CHURCH. With Twelve Plates and many Vignettes. Cloth, gilt edges, 16s.

Also a Large-paper Edition, with Proofs of the Plates. Price 42s. half morocco.

Specimen of the Minor Illustrations in 'Isis and Thamesis.'

OXFORD. Chapters by A. LANG. With Ten Etchings by A. Brunet-Debaines, A. Toussaint, and R. Kent Thomas, and several Vignettes. Price 1l. 1s.

'Told in Mr. Lang's best style, and beautifully illustrated.'—*Literary Churchman.*

LANDSCAPE. By PHILIP GILBERT HAMERTON, Author of 'Etching and Etchers,' 'The Graphic Arts,' &c. Columbier 8vo., with Fifty Illustrations, 5l. 5s.

Large-paper Copies, with Proofs of the Engravings, 10l. 10s.

'The superb volume before us may be said to represent, so far as this country is concerned, illustration, decoration, typography, and taste in binding at their best, employed on a work devoted to the fine arts exclusively.'—*Athenæum.*

THE GRAPHIC ARTS: A Treatise on the Varieties of Drawing, Painting, and Engraving. By PHILIP GILBERT HAMERTON. With Fifty-four Illustrations.

'This massive and authorative treatise on the technical part of almost every branch of art. . . . It is the masterpiece of Mr. Hamerton. . . . A beautiful work of lasting value.'—*Saturday Review.*

THE RUINED ABBEYS OF YORKSHIRE. By W. CHAMBERS LEFROY. With Twelve Etchings and numerous Vignettes. Price 1*l*. 1*s*.

'A very charming volume.'—*Leeds Mercury*.

EDINBURGH. Etchings from Drawings by S. Bough, R.S.A., and W. E. Lockhart, R.S.A. Vignettes by Hector Chalmers. Text by ROBERT LOUIS STEVENSON. Price 18*s*.

'Altogether a very charming gift-book.'—*Pall Mall Gazette*.

Specimen of the Illustrations in 'Early Flemish Artists.'

EARLY FLEMISH ARTISTS, AND THEIR PREDECESSORS ON THE LOWER RHINE. By W. M. CONWAY. With Twenty-nine Illustrations. Price 7*s*. 6*d*. cloth.

THE ARTISTIC DEVELOPMENT OF REYNOLDS AND GAINSBOROUGH. By W. M. CONWAY. With Sixteen Illustrations. Price 5*s*. cloth, gilt edges.

FINE ART BOOKS.

SCHOOLS OF MODERN ART IN GERMANY.
By J. BEAVINGTON ATKINSON. With Fifteen Etchings and numerous Woodcuts. Price 1*l.* 11*s.* 6*d.* Large-paper Copies, with Plates on India paper, price 3*l.* 3*s.*

'In every respect worthy of its subject.'—*Athenæum.*

THE ABBEY CHURCH OF ST. ALBANS. By J. W. COMYNS CARR. Illustrated with Five Etchings by Ernest George and R. Kent Thomas, and many smaller Illustrations. Price 18*s.*

'A bright, comprehensive history of the Abbey, with beautiful etchings and many woodcuts.'

LIFE OF ALBERT DÜRER. By Mrs. CHARLES HEATON. New Edition. With Portrait and Sixteen Illustrations. Price 10*s.* 6*d.*

'In its present form Mrs. Heaton's work deserves high commendation.'—*Guardian.*

ETCHINGS FROM THE NATIONAL GALLERY. Eighteen Plates by Flameng, Rajon, Le Rat, &c. With Notes by R. N. WORNUM. Large 4to. 1*l.* 11*s.* 6*d.* cloth, gilt edges.

ETCHINGS FROM THE NATIONAL GALLERY. Second Series. Eighteen Plates. Text by R. N. WORNUM. 1*l.* 11*s.* 6*d.*

EIGHTEEN ETCHINGS BY ENGLISH, FRENCH, AND GERMAN ARTISTS. Comprising Plates by Seymour Haden, Ernest George, Brunet-Debaines, &c. With Notes by P. G. HAMERTON. Imperial 4to. 1*l.* 11*s.* 6*d.* cloth, gilt edges.

FRENCH ARTISTS OF THE PRESENT DAY. Twelve Facsimile Engravings after Pictures. With Notices of the Painters by RENE MENARD. Large 4to. 1*l.* 1*s.* cloth, gilt edges.

'A handsome and most interesting book.'—*Times.*

FLAXMAN'S CLASSICAL OUTLINES. Cheap Edition for the use of Schools of Designs. With Notes by J. C. L. SPARKES, Head Master of the National Art Training Schools, South Kensington. 14*s.* complete, cloth.

THE SYLVAN YEAR: Leaves from the Note-Book of Raoul Dubois. By P. G. HAMERTON. With Twenty Etchings, by the Author and other Artists. 8vo. 12*s.* 6*d.* cloth. Cheap Edition, with Eight Etchings. Price 5*s.*

CHAPTERS ON ANIMALS. By P. G. HAMERTON. With Twenty Etchings. Post 8vo. 12*s.* 6*d.* cloth. Cheap Edition, with Eight Etchings. Price 5*s.*

BOOKS FOR PRESENTS

A CANTERBURY PILGRIMAGE. Ridden, Written, and Illustrated by JOSEPH & ELIZABETH PENNELL. Price 1s.; cloth, gilt edges, 2s. 6d.

> 'The most wonderful shillingsworth that modern literature has to offer.'
> —*Daily News.*

AN ITALIAN PILGRIMAGE. By Mrs. PENNELL. With many Illustrations by J. Pennell. Price 6s. cloth.

Specimen of the Illustrations in 'An Italian Pilgrimage.'

FLATLAND: A Romance of Many Dimensions. By A. SQUARE. Price 2s. 6d.

> 'This book is at once a popular scientific treatise of great value, and a fairy tale worthy to rank with "The Water Babies" and "Alice in Wonderland."'—*Oxford Magazine.*

SINTRAM AND HIS COMPANIONS. By DE LA MOTTE FOUQUE. A New Translation. With numerous Illustrations by Heywood Sumner. Cloth, price 5s.

JAMES HANNINGTON. First Bishop of Eastern Equatorial Africa. A Memoir. By the Rev. E. C. DAWSON, M.A. With Portrait, and Illustrations after the Bishop's own Sketches. Price 7s. 6d. cloth.

FOREST OUTLAWS; OR, ST. HUGH AND THE KING. By the Rev. E. GILLIAT. With Sixteen Illustrations. Price 5s. cloth.

HORACE WALPOLE AND HIS WORLD. Select passages from his Letters. With Eight copper-plates after Sir Joshua Reynolds and Sir Thomas Lawrence. Cloth, price 6s. Also a Large-paper Edition, with Proofs of the Plates, price 12s. 6d.

FATHER ALDUR: a Water Story. By A. GIBERNE. With Sixteen Tinted Illustrations. Price 5s. cloth.

AMONG THE STARS; OR, WONDERFUL THINGS IN THE SKY. By A. GIBERNE. With Illustrations. *Third Thousand.* Price 5s.

SUN, MOON, AND STARS. A Book on Astronomy for Beginners. By A. GIBERNE. With Coloured Illustrations. *Twelfth Thousand.* Cloth, price 5s.

'Ought to have a place in village libraries and mechanics' institutions; would also be welcome as a prize-book.'—*Pall Mall Gazette.*

THE WORLD'S FOUNDATIONS. Geology for Beginners. By A. GIBERNE. With Illustrations. *Third Thousand.* Cloth, price 5s.

'The exposition is clear, the style simple and attractive.'—*Spectator.*

MODERN FRENCHMEN. Five Biographies. By P. G. HAMERTON. Post 8vo. 7s. 6d. cloth.

I. VICTOR JACQUEMONT.
II. HENRY PERREYVE.
III. FRANCOIS RUDE.
IV. JEAN JACQUES AMPERE.
V. HENRI REGNAULT.

ROUND MY HOUSE. Notes of Rural Life in France in Peace and War. *Third Edition.* 5s. cloth.

A SHORT HISTORY OF NAPOLEON THE FIRST. By Professor SEELEY. With Portrait. Price 5s. cloth.

'Within the limits which the author has set himself the essay seems to us one of singular force and brilliancy.'—*Guardian.*

STORIES OF THE MAGICIANS. By Professor A. J. CHURCH. With Coloured Illustrations. Price 5s. cloth.

WITH THE KING AT OXFORD. By Professor A. J. CHURCH. With Coloured Illustrations. Price 5s. cloth.

THE CHANTRY PRIEST OF BARNET: a Tale of the Two Roses. By Professor A. J. CHURCH. With Coloured Illustrations, price 5s.

STORIES FROM THE CLASSICS. By the Rev. A. J. CHURCH, M.A., Professor of Latin at University College, London. With Coloured Illustrations.

STORIES FROM HOMER. 5s.
STORIES FROM VIRGIL. 5s.
STORIES FROM THE GREEK TRAGEDIANS. 5s.
STORIES OF THE EAST FROM HERODOTUS. 5s.
THE STORY OF THE PERSIAN WAR. 5s.
STORIES FROM LIVY. 5s.
ROMAN LIFE IN THE DAYS OF CICERO. 5s.
THE STORY OF THE LAST DAYS OF JERUSALEM. 3s. 6d.
A TRAVELLER'S TRUE TALE FROM LUCIAN. 3s. 6d.
HEROES AND KINGS. 1s. 6d.

BORDER LANCES. By the Author of 'Belt and Spur.' With Coloured Illustrations. Price 5s.

BELT AND SPUR. Stories of the Knights of Old. By the same Author. *Third Thousand.* With Sixteen Illuminations. Cloth, price 5s.

'A sort of boys' Froissart, with admirable illustrations.'—*Pall Mall Gazette.*

THE CITY IN THE SEA. Stories of the Old Venetians. By the Author of 'Belt and Spur.' With Coloured Illustrations. Cloth, price 5s.

STORIES OF THE ITALIAN ARTISTS FROM VASARI. By the Author of 'Belt and Spur.' With Coloured Illustrations, price 5s. cloth.

THE PHARAOHS AND THEIR LAND: Scenes of Old Egyptian Life and History. By E. BERKLEY. With Coloured Illustrations. Cloth, price 5s.

'An account of that wonderful land which is not only interesting, but valuable.'—*Leeds Mercury.*

Specimen of the Illustrations in 'Stories of the Italian Painters.'

BOOKS FOR PRESENTS

SUE; OR, WOUNDED IN SPORT. By E. VINCENT BRITON, Author of 'Amyot Brough.' Price 1s. sewed; 1s. 6d. cloth.

'Shows both pathos and humour. Sue and her lover Abner are fine figures, and the easy Monroe household is a forcibly satirical sketch.'
Pall Mall Gazette.

AMYOT BROUGH. By E. VINCENT BRITON. With Illustrations. Price 5s. cloth.

'With national pride we dwell on a beautiful English historical novel ... this sweet unpretending story, with its pretty engravings.'—*Academy.*

THE TOWER ON THE CLIFF: a Legend. By EMMA MARSHALL, Author of 'Under the Mendips,' &c. Price 1s. sewed; 1s. 6d. cloth.

'Founded on an old legend attaching to a Gloucestershire castle, which has afforded the authoress material for working up a romantic story.'—*Times.*

Specimen of the Illustrations in 'Australia.'

AUSTRALIA; OR, ENGLAND IN THE SOUTH. By G. SUTHERLAND, M.A., of Melbourne University. With Illustrations. Price 1s. sewed; 1s. 6d. cloth.

'A very interesting and instructive little work.'—*Times.*

CHAPTERS ON FLOWERS. By CHARLOTTE ELIZABETH. A New Edition, with Coloured Illustrations. Price 5s. cloth.

TALES by MISS CHARLESWORTH.

MINISTERING CHILDREN. 5s., 2s. 6d., 1s., or 6d.
A SEQUEL TO 'MINISTERING CHILDREN.' 5s. or 2s. 6d.
THE MINISTRY OF LIFE. 5s.
SUNDAY AFTERNOONS IN THE NURSERY. 2s. 6d.

THE OLD LOOKING-GLASS. 2s. 6d.
THE BROKEN LOOKING-GLASS. 2s. 6d.
OLIVER OF THE MILL. 5s.
ENGLAND'S YEOMEN. 5s. or 2s. 6d.

TALES by MISS GIBERNE.

DUTIES AND DUTIES. 5s.
THE CURATE'S HOME. 5s.
THE RECTOR'S HOME. 5s.
SWEETBRIAR. 5s.
FLOSS SILVERTHORN. 3s. 6d.
WILL FOSTER OF THE FERRY. 2s. 6d.

MURIEL BERTRAM. 5s.
THE BATTLEFIELD OF LIFE. 5s.
COULYNG CASTLE. 5s.
THE HILLSIDE CHILDREN. 3s. 6d.
NOT FORSAKEN. 2s. 6d.
THE DAY-STAR. 2s. 6d.

TALES by MRS. MARSHALL.

CONSTANTIA CAREW. 5s.
MEMORIES OF TROUBLOUS TIMES. 5s.
THE ROCHEMONTS. 5s.
LADY ALICE. 5s.
LIFE'S AFTERMATH. 5s.
A LILY AMONG THORNS. 5s.
HEIGHTS AND VALLEYS. 5s.
HELEN'S DIARY. 5s.
CHRISTABEL KINGSCOTE. 5s.
THE OLD GATEWAY. 5s.
BENVENUTA. 5s.
IN THE EAST COUNTRY. 5s.
THE MISTRESS OF TAYNE COURT. 5s.

DOROTHY'S DAUGHTERS. 5s.
JOB SINGLETON'S HEIR. 5s.
JOANNA'S INHERITANCE. 5s.
NOWADAYS. 5s.
MRS. MAINWARING'S JOURNAL. 5s.
BROTHERS AND SISTERS. 5s.
EDWARD'S WIFE. 5s.
VIOLET DOUGLAS. 5s.
MILLICENT LEGH. 5s.
IN COLSTON'S DAYS. 5s.
MRS. WILLOUGHBY'S OCTAVE. 5s.
UNDER THE MENDIPS. 5s.
IN FOUR REIGNS. 5s.

TALES by MISS WINCHESTER.

A NEST OF SPARROWS. 5s.
A WAYSIDE SNOWDROP. 3s. 6d.
CHIRP WITH THE CHICKS. 2s. 6d.
A CRIPPLED ROBIN. 5s.

UNDER THE SHIELD. 5s.
THE CABIN ON THE BEACH. 5s.
A CITY VIOLET, 5s.
A SEA PEARL. 5s.

FOR THE YOUNG.

CHURCH ECHOES: a Tale Illustrative of the Daily Service of the Prayer-book. By Mrs. CAREY BROCK, Author of 'Sunday Echoes in Week-day Hours.' Price 5s. cloth.

'Will be found very useful in leading thoughtful young people to an intelligent use of their Prayer-book.'—*Guardian.*

By the same Author.

CHANGES AND CHANCES. 5s.	THE RECTORY AND THE MANOR. 5s.
WORKING AND WAITING. 5s.	
MARGARET'S SECRET. 5s.	HOME MEMORIES. 5s.
CHARITY HELSTONE. 5s.	THE VIOLETS OF MONTMARTRE. 5s.
MICHELINE. 5s.	
MY FATHER'S HAND. 2s.	DAME WYNTON. 3s. 6d.
CHILDREN AT HOME. 5s.	ALMOST PERSUADED. 1s.

SUNDAY ECHOES IN WEEKDAY HOURS. A Series of Illustrative Tales. Eight Vols. 5s. each.

1. The Collects.
2. The Church Catechism.
3. Journey of the Israelites.
4. Scripture Characters.
5. The Epistles and Gospels.
6. The Parables.
7. The Miracles.
8. The Example of Christ.

900th Thousand.

THE CHILDREN'S HYMN-BOOK. Edited by Mrs. CAREY BROCK, and Revised by Bishop W. WALSHAM HOW, Bishop OXENDEN, Rev. J. ELLERTON.

A. Royal 32mo. price 1d. sewed ; 2d. cloth extra.
B. Royal 32mo. price 1s. cloth ; 1s. 6d. cloth extra.
C. With Music, price 3s. cloth ; 3s. 6d. cloth extra.

The book contains 387 hymns, 13 litanies, and 20 carols, with many new tunes by eminent composers. It has called forth the following opinions from

The late ARCHBISHOP OF CANTERBURY.

'The selection of hymns is obviously a most excellent one, and I hope that the book may become very popular. I wish you every success in the results of your important labours.'

BISHOP OF WINCHESTER.

'I found your beautiful book on my return from Confirmation. I like extremely all that I see of the book, and trust it will be a great success.'

BISHOP OF ELY.

'It seems to me excellently adapted to meet the requirements of children.'

BISHOP OF WORCESTER.

'I shall feel much confidence in recommending it for general use in the Diocese of Worcester.'

www.ingramcontent.com/pod-product-compliance
Lightning Source LLC
Chambersburg PA
CBHW030019240426
43672CB00007B/1009